Growing up under Montserrat's sleeping Volcano[*]: memories from a colonial childhood on a British Caribbean island 1952-61

by
David R. Bradshaw

"That is the land of lost content,
I see it shining plain,
The happy highways where I went
And cannot come again."
(A.E Housman: (1859-1936) *Last Poems* (1922), 6, Lancer)

---

[*] In fact, as Dr Howard A. Fergus tells us in his chapter entitled *"Soufrieres and Volcanoes in Our History"*, from the book *"Eruption[:] Montserrat versus Volcano"* edited by himself (1996), at page 13, Montserrat contains several volcanoes, as follows: *"The island is made up of seven masses, each representing an erupted volcano. From north to south they are Silver Hill (1,200 feet), Centre Hills (2,450), Garibaldi Hill (840 feet), St George's Hill (1,200 feet), Soufriere Hills, peaking at (3,002 feet) at Mount Chance, South Soufriere Hills (2,505) feet and Roache's Bluff (1,230 feet). ...Silver Hill was probably the first to erupt while the Soufriere Hills are the youngest".* The "Volcano" referred to in the title of this book is the said youngest, and no longer sleeping (since 18 July,1995), Soufriere Hills one which is to be found in the southern half of Montserrat.

Dedicated to the memory of
Joanna, my late <u>great</u>-
grandmother; and for "Meena",
my early (and still great) wife.

Published in the United Kingdom by

Montserratian (in Cambridgeshire) Publishing
12 Pryor Close
Old School Lane
Milton
CAMBRIDGE CB24 6BU
davidRbradshaw@yahoo.com

A CIP catalogue record of this book is available from the British Library

First printed November 2010

Cover design by Natalia Maca

ISBN: 978-0-9565929-0-3

Preface

"Everyone has a book in them!" Thus goes the usual (if grammatically incorrect) refrain, which I have heard from time to time for most of my adult life. Indeed, for many years, I have felt that I had one in me too. But what could I write about? A related statement in this context is: "Write about what you know". So, when finally I decided to stop keeping my book "inside" me and to get it out on paper, I decided to write about what I knew *best*. Myself!

I have always thought that I have had a remarkable life story to tell. Most autobiographers probably start out feeling much the same way! But what I thought made my own history "different" was not simply the fact that my parents left me behind to be cared for by one of their relatives, when they decided to emigrate from our native Caribbean island of Montserrat, for England, in the early 1950s. (For lots of other indigenous West Indian parents were doing exactly the same thing as mine, at more or less the same time – and beyond, up to the 1960s and, possibly, even after that). Rather, what I thought made my biography "out of the ordinary" was because of *who* the relative taking care of me was. Not the usual paternal or maternal grandmother. Instead, in my case, it was *my mother's* own *grand*mother! Moreover, the impetus to tell my tale was all the more compelling because of the remarkably strong character of that elderly lady - in taking on such an onerous task of childrearing when, as a then old-age pensioner, she should have been putting her feet up and "slowing down" in life! So important, indeed, is that exceptional lady to my story that I seriously toyed with the idea of making a play on the title of Edith Clarke's famous book[†] and calling my own: "My *Great-grand*mother who fathered me"!

There is something else, too, which adds some piquancy, and an uncommonness, to the story of my early life. This is the fact that, for most of my three score years or so on this Earth, I have harboured a deep and personal secret from my childhood days. I have kept it locked away in my innermost consciousness, and this suppression, or repression, process could not have done me much good over so long a period. Some 50 years on, therefore, it seems to me high time that this secret be confronted, full on – and any demons relating to it slain, once and for all. What could be better, therefore, than to make such "confrontation" as complete as possible by ensuring that it happens as publicly as I reasonably can – that is to say, within the pages of this, my first, book? But, as will be seen, perhaps, the foregoing sentence is somewhat "easier said (or written) than done"!

In fact, however, this book is not just about me, or my great-grandmother. It is more about "us" – me and my younger brother, John. He, my "Bro J" (as I affectionately call him

---

[†] "*My Mother Who Fathered Me: a study of the families in three selected communities of Jamaica*" (University of the West Indies Press, Kingston, Jamaica, 1999 – first edition 1957)

these days), was with me every step of the way – from the time that I could first remember anything at all of my childhood in Montserrat.

I thank my Bro J, therefore, for his fraternal companionship in that early journey of ours in our native "Emerald Isle of the West Indies" – and for, more recently, reading the manuscript (MS) of this book and generally concluding: "Yes, Bro D! That's how it was". His steadfast support, and belief in me, as I took up my new writing "career" has been invaluable to me and I cannot thank him enough for that.

I also wish to thank, most sincerely, another person for their undying support and belief in my getting started, and continuing, on the road to recording "How it was". That person is Dr C. Studd – who always thought that the title of this book should simply be *"BAREFOOT"*, and to whom the finalised version is a continuing tribute. Another doctor is Anne – my family physician – who must be thanked, too, for reading my MS not once but twice! And, moreover, for then giving me the most unexpected and effusive praise and encouragement relating to it. "Life enhancing – or, even, saving" is the expression which readily comes to mind as a result of her kindness to me in this regard – and I thank her again for it as sincerely as I can. The same profuse thanks also go to Mrs Leila Gordon, who was the caring, wise and empathetic person who put me on to Professor Alice Miller and the various editions of the latter's famous book, *"Drama of the Child"*[‡]. As may be discovered within the pages of this book, those earlier volumes of Professor Miller have had the most profound impact on my "new life" in this first decade of the recently-begun Millennium! Both Leila, and her

---

[‡] See footnote 2, in Chapter 1 below, and the text relating thereto

colleague, Dr Wendy Croft, agreed to read an early draft of this book and I am most grateful to them for doing so and for their encouragement in my undertaking the enterprise. One last "professional" also deserves my heartfelt thanks for her encouragement to me after reading an early draft of this book. She is Ms Louise Brennand, my optician. When I doubted that I had any abilities at all as a writer, "Lou" gave me fresh hope in pursuing my efforts in that direction – and for that I am deeply grateful.

In the early days of typing the MS of this book, I used the services of the Cambridgeshire County Council (Public) Libraries in the village of Linton and, in particular, those of Librarian there, Mrs Linda Pearson, who very kindly later read, and commented on, an early draft of the MS. Indeed, it was Mrs Pearson who kindly suggested that I would be better off using the greater range of services available from Essex County Council (Public) Libraries in the lovely town of Saffron Walden - a mere six miles away, but over the county border, from Linton. I duly followed her advice and in "SW" made much progress on the MS, thanks to all the friendly librarian staff whom I encountered there – including (but not limited to) Mrs Jill Palmer, Mrs Sara Willard, Heather, Ruth, Christine, Roz, Glenda and Roger (especially for the "extra time" on the library's scanner and PCs which they so regularly gave me during 2008). Mrs Palmer even went to the trouble of reading an early draft of the MS and giving me some verbal suggestions for its improvement, for which I remain very grateful (as I also am to the rest of her wonderful staff). Another person situated within the Saffron Walden Library (in the Essex Record Office, Archive Access Point) was most encouraging to me with my project and even arranged for a colleague of hers to teach me the rudiments of how to distinguish between "first", "second", "third etc" cousins on the one hand, and cousins who are "once removed", "twice removed" or "three times removed etc" on the other. The lady in question is Mrs Zofia Everett. For her kindness, and educational services, I shall remain ever thankful.

More recently, I have been trying to turn my "sow's ear", earliest, MS into something more suitable for publication, in the Digital Resources Area (DRA) of the University Library of Cambridge University (UL). Mr Phiwe Mtwebana, the kind gentleman in day-to-day charge of the DRA, has been the most helpful, and patient, computer expert that I could ever have wished for to assist me with my task of setting my memories down in permanent form. I will forever be grateful for the help, encouragement and laughs which he provided me with – always happily - along the way. Out of all our many exchanges, a firm (and long-lasting) friendship between us has (I am willing to trust) been born. (Phiwe's recent successors in the UL, Ben and Rachel (and their Research Skills etc Librarian colleague, "Dr Emma"), have been most helpful, too, in assisting me to revise the proofs of this volume – and I thank them for that, and their patience with me, too).

My heartfelt thanks also go out across the Atlantic Ocean to two cousins of mine back in my native Caribbean. First, to Mrs Beverley Mendes, my first cousin (once removed) - and her lovely family – who kindly hosted me in her home in Woodlands, Montserrat in February 2010. Through Beverley's liaison with her own cousin on her mother's side, Ms Sedrica Chambers (to whom I am eternally grateful, also, and extend my thanks) I was helped to discover my great-grandmother Joanna's age at her death and, thereby and finally (after years of searching), just how old she was when she took Bro J and myself on, and in, during the mid-1950s. The other cousin, again originating from my father's (and his father's) Dyers district of central Montserrat, is Ms Eulalie Greenaway – a fellow lawyer, who now teaches would-be members of our profession at the Mona Campus of the University of the West Indies (UWI) in Kingston, Jamaica. I thank her for (inadvertently, perhaps?!) assisting me to re-discover the identity of "Mr P" - a central character in this book and perhaps, also, in my life's history! Eulalie helped me through the good offices of our fellow-countryman back in Montserrat, Mr Oris Sullivan - for whose invaluable assistance I extend my deepest gratitude. Also situated in Jamaica is Mrs Linda Speth, General Manager of the UWI Press based at Mona, Kingston. Linda not only took time to read an early draft of the MS of this book in 2008, but also met with me at Mona in February 2010 to give me painstaking instructions on how I might best go about self-publishing the work. For her encouragement and guidance, I thank her most sincerely.

In Montserrat itself, on Tuesday 23 February 2010, I interviewed (along with Cousin Beverley) a wonderful, and venerable, lady of a certain age! She was blind, but full of *joie de vivre*. In fact, she was aged 87 years old and, so she told me, "the very last of the 26 children of [her] father" – one James Bradshaw of Salem, the brother of my paternal grandfather, Joseph of Dyers. Her name is *Miss* (and she emphasised her non-marital status to me, more than once, during our interview) Catherine Bradshaw. I am immensely grateful to her for the memories which she recounted to me, and for the lively manner in which she did so. Meeting Cousin Catherine, and conversing with her, was another one of those life-enhancing moments of my life and I thank her for the experience. Similar thanks go out to her fellow residents at the Golden Years Nursing Home in Montserrat who allowed me to interview them on that late February day in question – namely, Mr "Papa Jackie", and his pal Mr Walter Lindo - both "old boys" from the Kinsale area, just below Amersham (and "the Volcano") where my Bro J and I grew up.

Whilst in Montserrat in February 2010, Cousin Beverley introduced me briefly to another lady who was to have a major impact on my life and my ability to research "Montserratians things" in order to complete this book. That other lady was Ms Rose Willock OBE, one of the leading broadcasters on our island's Radio Montserrat (otherwise known as "ZJB Radio"). I cannot thank Rose enough for all the "leads" she has given me about Magistrates of Montserrat in the 1950s and 1960s, past Governors and their wives, many other matters relating to the book, and (above all) for being the most faithful and encouraging of my Montserrat correspondents.

My cousin, Ernest Bradshaw, and his family in Antigua (Montserrat's near-neighbour-island) very kindly facilitated my comfortable transfer, and over-night stay *en route*, in my getting from Eulalie in Jamaica to Beverley in Montserrat during early 2010 and I am immensely grateful to him and his wife and children for the exceptional kindness and hospitality which they showed me.

Closer to my home in my adopted country, I wish to thank my late father's surviving brothers and their only sister (most of whom live in London) for all their help which required their searching their respective memory banks about life "back home" in Montserrat in bygone days - stretching back to the first quarter of the 20th century in some cases. I refer to my Uncles Willy (now 89 years old), Tom (now 81) and Hammy (now 78). Their older sister, Mary (now 92) – my "Auntie Martin" – is, perhaps, the one member of my father's siblings who could tell me most about "the old days" in, and around, the Dyers community of Montserrat. Alas, though I try to visit, and "talk with", her at least once a month in the Mary Seacole Nursing Home in Hackney, London where she now resides, she suffered a severe stroke in early 2008 – shortly before I commenced the research for, and writing of, this book. She has not, therefore, been able to contribute to the family history facts contained in its last chapter – but, nevertheless, I take this golden opportunity to thank her now for all that she has done for me, and all the widely-spread Bradshaw family, during the nearly one century span of her life. (Just before this book went to print, sadly, Auntie Martin passed away – on the unforgettable date of 10.10.10, or the 10th of October 2010. May you rest in peace, dear Auntie – forever!)

In the same sincere vein, I also thank all my other family members who, in any way, contributed to my telling of the family story, and history, in this book – whether that be the parts relating to my late father's or late mother's respective sides. In conveying these sentiments of gratitude, I intend to include (but am not limiting myself to): Mrs Gloria Meade (*née* Bradshaw), her mother (and, simultaneously, my aunt by marriage and great-aunt by blood) Mrs Amelia Bradshaw; Mrs Elaine ("Mem") Daley (for being the family's helpful "oracle") and her husband Joe; Mrs Ann ("Nan") Irish and her husband, also called Joe (and their daughter, Hyacinth, who just "couldn't wait" to see the first "proof" of this book and who read it (at one sitting!) in July 2010 and gave me much positive, and creative, feedback afterwards); Mrs Charlotte Richardson and her husband - again also called Joe; my late "Uncle" Ben's two brothers, Messrs John and George White (and John's wife, Sarah); Pastor Danny Bradshaw; Mrs Doris Shepherd (especially for her remarkably long memories about our joint Bradshaw family history, despite her only having lived in Dyer's, Montserrat for just two short periods as a small girl); Cousin Beverley's mother, Mrs Daisy Ryan (*aka* Bradshaw); Cousin "Par-pa" in Swindon, Wiltshire (more formally known as Emmanuel Joseph Cabey); and last – but, certainly, by no means least - my Godmother, Mrs Maude Brandt (*née* Herbert). I am, and will remain, ever grateful to each and every one of these kinfolk, and kind folk, of mine.

To Adrian Ray, too, I tender my gratitude – for often being my fellow-self-publisher and neighbouring writer and researcher in the UL, for steering me though the choppy waters of how to acquire one's own ISBN number and proceed along the road to making one's writings available to the world at large, for proofreading (with his wife, Mandy?) this book in its final stages, and for warning me against "strangers bearing gifts"! Another "neighbour" of mine in the UL is Dr Christine Corton and I also thank her, too, for agreeing, at the eleventh hour, to proof-read the 2010 redraft of my MS and for all the encouragement she gave me in that connection.

I am profoundly obliged to Iroshan, the "supremo" of Fencabs of Ely, Cambridgeshire, England for allowing me to satisfy my "social conscience" each school day – and for providing me with the vehicle from which I can also attempt to launch my new life as a writer. If "out of small acorns, great oaks can grow" then, maybe, out of a diminutive Skoda…!

Last, but by no means least, I thank my wife and children for supporting me during the two, and more, years' journey that it has taken me to travel from the *thought* of writing my early memoirs to actually seeing them appear in print. I know that I have not always been easy to live with along the way – and that that is a mere euphemism for "how it was"!

Finally, I wish to dedicate this book to two of the most important ladies in my life: Joanna, my late, and literally "great", maternal great-grandmother; and "Meena", my very much extant, and also (in every sense) "great", wife. Without them, I would not have been here to tell the tale!

D.R.B

Milton village, Cambridgeshire;
and the University Library, Cambridge, England
October 2010

Contents

Chapter 1: Introducing: Myself, Montserrat and "Joanna"   **1**

(a) Enter David!   *1*
(b) Montserrat   *2*
(c) More about myself (and my little brother, John)   *11*
(d) Joanna (and Maas Bab)   *18*

Chapter 2: Schooldays in Montserrat   **46**

(a) Barefoot Boys and our school   *46*
(b) Early crime!   *49*
(c) Into the Juniors (and the private school)   *52*
(d) Brother John starts school   *55*
(e) My "starring" roles   *56*
(f) Death to a schoolboy   *60*
(g) Outings to netball at Bathfield   *63*
(h) Childhood recreations   *65*

(i) "Colonials" celebrating and/or
    honouring the British Empire   72
(j) Masquerade   74
(k) A trip "abroad"   76
(l) Introducing "Mr P"   77
(m) "Doctors and nurses" (and beyond?) 90

Chapter 3: Taking Leave of My Sensible
Horizons   92

(a) Getting immunised and
    luggage-buying   92
(b) Presents <u>from</u> the teacher   94
(c) The ticket to travel and the acquiring of a
    minder for the passage   96
(d) The leaving of Joanna and Maas Bab 103
(e) Getting aboard, for abroad   105

Chapter 4: Back before the Future   114

(a) My Father's extended (and "extensive")
    family   114
(b) The death of my paternal grandfather,
    Joseph, and the marriage of my parents 123
(c) Further introducing Dad's brother, Tom 130
(d) The travels of my father   133
(e) The original coming together of my parents,
    and their first transatlantic "separation" 141
(f) Dad "finds his feet" in England; and
    a new baby in his arms   153

Chapter 1:
Introducing: Myself, Montserrat and "Joanna"

(a) Enter David!

Out I popped, head first I presume, on the eighteenth day of September 1952. Thus, as my mother's first-born and (very likely) her most painfully produced offspring, I appeared to face the world - ready to make the first cry of many which would leave my lungs and mouth, often, throughout my future life. So, you might say, I started that life with a "down"! There was only one direction to go to after that.

Such appearance of mine took place on the Caribbean island of Montserrat. More precisely, my birth certificate states that I, David Reinford Bradshaw, was born at Ryner's Village on that island, to my father James Alfred Bradshaw, "Labourer" of the said village, and my mother Margaret Ann. It also states that I was born "Legitimate", since my parents were stated as being "Married", and that I was of the "Male" sex. The informant of my birth to Acting Registrar Allan F.G.L. Louisy, on 22 September 1952, was one Edith Griffith.

(b) Montserrat

But where on earth is this island of Montserrat? It is in fact one of many in an arc of islands which begin about 90 miles south of the Florida Keys, with Cuba as the northern outpost, and which continue in a roughly south-easterly direction for hundreds of miles until the island of Trinidad - which lies a mere nine miles north of Venezuela, on the South American mainland, at the closest point: see Fig 1 below. If we zoom in on this arc of islands about half way along its length (see Fig 2 below), we find Montserrat situated between Antigua to the north-east, the islands of St Kitts and Nevis to the north-west and the French "overseas department" island of Guadeloupe to the south-east.

In further introducing Montserrat and obtaining just a little flavour of some of its attributes and local colour, one could do a lot worse than quote the (not wholly-kind) remarks about the island's tiny size and population, and some of its foibles, made by a former London Stipendiary Magistrate and Barrister, one Mr Eric Crowther - who acted as the only Magistrate on Montserrat for three months in 1996. For, when speaking of his experiences on the island during his tenure, Mr Crowther wrote, among other things, as follows (in the British journal *Justice of the Peace and Local Government Law* for 6 November 1996, at pages 979 to 980, entitled "DUELS IN THE SUN"):

"And so I find myself on Montserrat. It is in the West Indies and can be discovered among the Leeward Islands by those with a powerful magnifying glass. It is about 77 square miles [sic] in area but this has been reduced to about nine square miles [sic!] by the activities of the volcano, which erupted fiercely in April of this year and has been simmering gently - and often not so gently - ever since. The population has reduced in the last six months from about 11,000 to about 7,000, many living in churches and schools. Plymouth, the capital, and a large part of the island is now an 'evacuated area' [see Figs 3 and 4 below] while people are not allowed to re-enter without the express permission of the Governor….

English common law is the basis of Montserrat law but there are many differences…. [For example, there] is a different approach to some offences … [from] that which obtains in the United Kingdom.

Whilst one of two men who shot at my predecessor received only seven years when convicted of attempting to murder her (she does seem to have been universally popular) a man who had sexual relations with a donkey received 11 years (he should not have been such an ass). Drunken driving is not regarded at all seriously, unless it results in death, whereas the taking of cannabis is gravely regarded and there are numerous prosecutions for indecent language. The use of the 'f'-word seems to be very much frowned upon in Montserrat. When a (very skilful) photographer appeared before me on four separate charges of using the 'f'-word last year (his trial was delayed because he wanted to be represented and the lawyers were all on strike), I felt a sense of outrage in the court when I suggested that rather than have a trial which was estimated to last two days, the defendant might agree to be bound over. When the tumult died down a little, I sought to justify my proposal by saying, 'Well, shortly before coming here, I heard that word used many times in one evening on the B.B.C'. There was a shout from the public gallery: 'Then the B.B.C. ought to be prosecuted'. On reflection, I am inclined to agree."

David R. Bradshaw

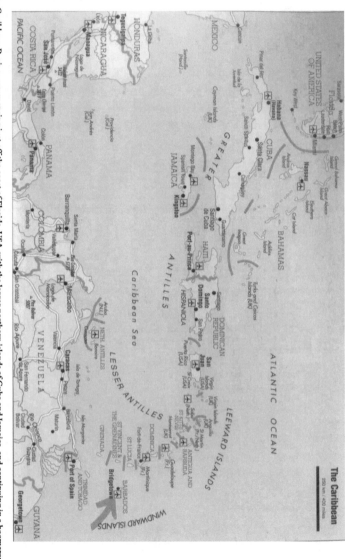

Fig 1: The Caribbean Region, commencing just off the coast of Florida, USA, with the larger northern islands of Cuba and Jamaica, and continuing in a boomerang or "arc" shape south-eastwards until the islands of Trinidad and Tobago and ending with Venezuela on the South American mainland. The map is taken from "Insight Pocket Guide BARBADOS", published by APA Publications (UK) Ltd. Used under licence.

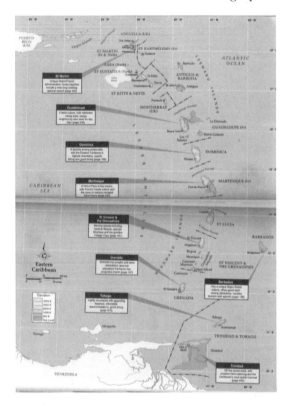

Fig 2: The Eastern Caribbean, showing the biggest "curve" in the "arc" formed by the islands of the Caribbean region (shown in Fig 1 above), and depicting, among other things, the Leeward Islands group and Montserrat's position in that group (just to the north-west of the well-flagged, butterfly-shaped, island of Guadeloupe). (Map used with the kind permission of Lonely Planet Publications, Hawthorn, Vic 3122, Australia: www.lonelyplanet.com).

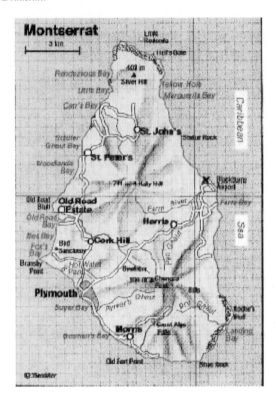

Fig 3: Montserrat, as it was before the 1995 Soufriere Hills volcanic eruption – that is to say, as it would have been during the author's boyhood years on the island between 1952 and 1961. Map courtesy of <u>www.theodora.com/maps</u>, and is used with permission.

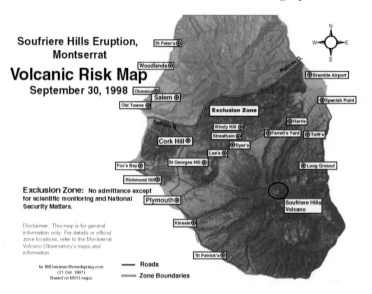

Fig 4: Montserrat, as the main expanse of the island became after the 1995 Soufriere Hills volcanic eruption – showing not only the site of the Volcano itself but also the nearby locations of, among other places, Plymouth, Kinsale and Dyer's - which locations will feature very largely in the present volume. (Map used with the kind permission of Mr Bill Innanen. Email: Bill.Innanen@mindspring.com)

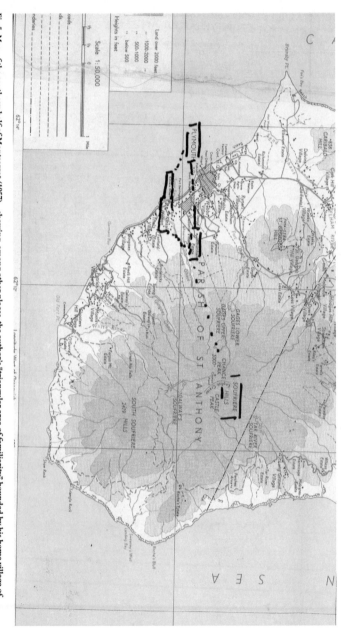

Fig 5: Map of the southern half of Montserrat (1957) – showing, among other places, the author's "triangular area of familiarity" bounded by his home village of Amersham, the island's capital of Plymouth, and his "sea-bathing" village of Kinsale. The map also shows the nearness of the Soufriere Hills – site of the 1995 Volcano – to Amersham and the "threat of danger" under which he and his brother John, unknowingly, spent their early childhoods. (Reproduced from the 1957 Ordnance Survey map).

When I appeared in the world of 1952 Montserrat, the volcano mentioned in Eric Crowther's article had already been lying dormant for some 400 years - as I understand it[1]. Moreover, in the 1950s, Montserrat, like so many of the other islands around it, was still a British colony. Most of those other islands, including nearby Antigua, Barbuda, St Kitts, Nevis, Dominica, St Lucia and Barbados have all gone on to achieve their independence from the United Kingdom (whether individually or in partnership with a neighbouring island). Montserrat, however, is still a "colony" of sorts as I write in 2008. As such, it is a rarity in today's 21st century world - there being only 13 such "British Overseas Territories" (as such former British colonies are now re-labelled in a more "politically correct" fashion). In my year of birth, Montserrat's main town, and capital, was Plymouth - which tiny metropolis had been so since Georgian times, at least, and which finds itself situated at the south-western end of the island. Ryner's Village (see Fig 5 above), where my mother gave birth to me at home, is about one mile north-east of Plymouth - at a generous estimate. So I was

---

[1] Indeed, Dr Howard A Fergus, in his chapter entitled "*Soufrieres and Volcanoes in Our History*", in the book "*Eruption[:] Montserrat versus Volcano*" edited by himself (1996), at page 16, suggests that the last activity from any volcano in Montserrat had occurred much earlier than that, as follows: "*The island is said to have had its origins in volcanic action, but no eruption has occurred in historic time. The latest massive eruption with lava flows is thought to have taken place between 18,000 and 19,000 years ago, although there may have been a significant one just prior to the island's European colonisation in the 1630s.*" (Emphasis added). Dr Fergus cites, as his sources, the following: J.B. Shepherd, K. Rodney, L.Lynch, D. Beckles & W. Suite's "*Summary Proceedings of Lesser Antilles Volcanic Assessment Seminar*", University of the West Indies, St Augustine, Trinidad & Tobago, 1988, p,7; and P.E. Baker, "*Volcanic Hazards in St Kitts and Montserrat, West Indies*" Journal of the Geological Society, London, Vol. 142, 1985

David R. Bradshaw

something of a metropolitan boy from the very outset of my life!

Montserrat, W.I. Volcano

Fig 5A: A copy of a postcard showing the Soufriere Hills Volcano with its "Glowing Lava Dome [in] September 2006". © Kevin West, Paradise Photo and Art Studio, Montserrat, West Indies – and used with his kind permission.

(c) More about myself (and my little brother, John)

I do not, of course, remember my coming into the world in 1952. Nor, indeed, can I remember anything about my mother, Margaret, after my birth until many years beyond the age at which a child would normally be able to recall first being aware of its "mum". This is because, from the age of about two years, I was raised not by my own mother but, rather, by her mother's mother - that is to say, by my GREAT-grandmother! That venerable lady had the somewhat Dickensian-sounding name of Joanna Brumble. However, her first name was not pronounced as it would be in England - with the sounding of the two separate syllables of, firstly, "Jo" and then "Anna". Rather, in Montserrat we enunciated her name more like "Joan-nah" - or, even more vibrantly, with the first syllable stressed as in the Portuguese boy's name of *"João"* (or "John", in the English translation).

So the first question arises: why did my mother leave me to be brought up by a non-parent during my late infancy/early boyhood? The answer is that, like many other British Caribbean islanders in the 1950s, my parents must have decided that their family's economic prospects stood a better chance of improvement if they emigrated to jobs which were more plentiful in either North America or in Great Britain. My father, James, was to tell me in my late teens, or early twenties, about at least two periods in which he had spent time working temporarily in the United States around the time of my birth. If my memory serves me correctly, he mentioned apple-picking in Wisconsin in this connection. Perhaps, it was because of such not-very-productive experiences in America that he and my mother decided to leave instead for what, at that time, they perceived to be the greener pastures of the capital of the British Empire, and Montserrat's motherland - namely, London, England. Leaving little David behind - and, incidentally, his even smaller brother, John - whilst they emigrated in order to prepare a better "nest" in England before later reconstituting the full nuclear family unit in their newly-adopted country, must have appeared an attractive idea to my parents. This would have been particularly so if the separation from their two first-born children would only have been intended to be for a fairly temporary period and if the custody of those two boys could be left in the safe hands of a blood relation.

I have said that the separation took place when I was about two years old. In fact, I have always understood that my brother, John, was only 10 months old when my mother left us behind (with her grandmother, Joanna). This would, therefore, mean that it was about March 1955 when she emigrated - for John was born on the 10th of May 1954. Thus, at the time of that rupture in the relationship with my mother which I would have enjoyed with her since my birth, I would in fact have been just about two and a half years old. Not being knowledgeable about child development, it seems to me now that even at that tender age I should have retained a conscious memory of my mother from about that time. The plain fact is, however, that I have no such memory. It follows that, fortunately perhaps, neither do I possess any conscious memory of any sudden separation from the loving care of a mother for her 30-month old child – a care which, presumably, she would have lavished upon him, her first-born, constantly over the many months since his birth.

I should add, incidentally, that what applies in the case of the absence of an early memory of my mother equally applies (by greater reason) in relation to my father. For he had gone on ahead of my mother to England, presumably, in order to better prepare for her later arrival (after he had first seen to the acquisition of accommodation for his growing family and a job for himself). Thus, I had had an even shorter time to get to know my father before he had departed for the more economically attractive pastures of Merrye Olde England.

Of the very few pictures that I have ever seen from my childhood days in Montserrat, all of which few I now have in my possession as I write, there is one only which shows me alone (see Fig 6 below).

Fig. 6: Little David – at about 20 months of age?

It is in fact the earliest photograph which I have ever seen of myself and is the only one of those few which shows me without my younger brother John at my side. This could well mean that the photograph was taken before John was born, for it shows a small boy who could well be about, or less than, 20 months of age. That little boy is standing on a chair outside, what appears to be, a simple "chattel house" (which type of common Montserratian - and indeed Caribbean-wide - residence I will refer to in more detail later in this volume). He is wearing a pair of shoes, but it is noticeable that he is unsmiling and not appearing to be a particularly happy little soul. Is it not more likely, therefore, that the photograph was taken when I was at least two and a half years old? If so, perhaps my face shows that I was already (at that point in my relatively short life) keenly aware of the absence, or "loss", of my mother.

I have just referred to my present-day conscious memory being untouched by my mother's emigration. I now know, however, that I may well have been very traumatised by the sudden separation from her and that that experience could well have played - and perhaps is still playing - a major factor in my subconscious life and my mental development. In this connection, I refer to the theories of the psychoanalyst Alice Miller which are set out in her best-seller book "*The Drama of Being a Child: the Search for the True Self*" (1995)[2]. For example, Miller writes in her book (at pages 6 and 7):

"For millions of years, in the course of evolution, we have been programmed to offer loving care and protection to our new-born infants, and nature has equipped our young to receive only positive treatment. We do not have a natural mechanism for coping with mistreatment, nor can we erase it from our bodies, as everything that takes place in our lives remains registered in our cells as information. Nature gives us only the ability to anesthetize ourselves when

---

[2] Published by Virago, London 1995 – as translated by Ruth Ward from the original German: "*Das Drama des begabten Kindes*".

mistreatment becomes unbearable. Our organism protects itself…with the help of repression and denial".

Elsewhere in her book, Miller writes (at pages 2 and 14): *"The tragedy is that of early psychic injuries and their inevitable repression, which allows the child to survive. …As children, we had no choice but to learn the skills of repression in order to survive".* The author, and former member of the International Psychoanalytical Association, also tells us of the consequences of such childhood repression - in the following words (at pages 4 and 14): *"The repression of injuries endured during childhood is the root cause of psychic disorders and criminality. …If we don't have the courage to face the feelings we have repressed, however, they will continue to block our development and threaten our…health".* Finally, in a memorable passage – which Miller emphasises with her own italics – she reminds readers of her book that:

"We are all prisoners of our childhood, whether we know it, suspect it, deny it, or have never even heard about the possibility".

Since first writing the passage above, about the earliest extant photograph of myself at about 20 months old, a most amazing thing subsequently happened during a weekend in which I met with some of my relations in London for the purposes of my research for this volume - that is to say, on Saturday the 12th of April 2008. For, after I had returned home from my interviews that day, my brother John (who presently lives with his wife and my dear sister-in-law Sandra in the northern Caribbean country of Jamaica) casually told me in an email that he had in his possession a photograph of our mother holding a baby "in Ryner's Village", Montserrat. He also stated that he was unsure as to whether that baby was himself or me. At this piece of news, my excitement knew no bounds. For it possibly meant that my brother possessed the earliest photograph of myself which was still in existence - and one which I did not even know about or had ever set eyes upon, to the best of my knowledge. Accordingly, I immediately emailed him back and asked that he kindly scan the photograph in question and send it to me as an attachment to a further email from himself - as soon as possible! John, quickly complied with my urgent request.

When the photograph arrived I was truly amazed. This was because the photographer had taken it from outside the very (chattel) house in which the photograph in Fig 6 above had been taken. Moreover, the very chair on which I was standing in Fig 6 was in exactly the same place in the photo which John had just sent me - only, this time, my mother (who was holding an infant, of apparently no more than about a month or so) was sitting in that chair! Thus, the mystery of John's poser about the "baby in our Mum's arms" seemed solved. That baby was *not* me - although the photograph of me standing on the chair appears to have been taken at about the same time, from the same vantage point, and from the same angle as that of our mother holding the infant. That the baby in question is in fact my (very little) brother, John, seemed to be confirmed by my subsequent reference to my father's family bible (of which I will state a lot more in a later chapter). For, in the page about family baptisms, my father had himself completed details for my brother's as follows: "[Denzil] Fitzgerald Bradshaw …….31.5 1954" (see Fig 7 below). (I will explain, later on in Chapter 3, why no reference is made to the name "John" in my father's record making).

"All power in heaven and on earth
has been given to me. Go, therefore,
and make disciples of all nations,
baptizing them in the name of the
Father, and of the Son, and of the
Holy Spirit."

MATT. 28:18-19

ℬaptism

Our children, born to us in the flesh, were children of men. But through Baptism, in

which they were born again through water and the Holy Spirit, they became children of

God. The members of our family became members also of God's family.

David Rainford Bradshaw was baptized on *5-10-52* at *St. J. Roman Catholic Church*

The godparents were Maddie Raley *and* Miss Herbert

Densil Fitzgerald Bradshaw was baptized on *31-5-54* at *Plymouth Roman Catholic Church*

The godparents were Benjamin Aylmer *and* Miss Welch

Fig 7: Extract from Dad's family Bible showing the date of the Baptism of Baby John (then officially named "Denzil (or "Densil") Fitzgerald Bradshaw"

Given that the baby was dressed all in white, it is likely that the photo in question was taken to record the christening day of my baby brother in the very month of his birth. If this, seemingly, reasonable piece of speculation is correct, it would make my brother some three weeks old and me just about 20 months and two weeks of age. And whilst I was somewhat disappointed that the baby turned out not to be me and that my "glumness" (in the photo of me, standing on the common chair in question) was a natural personality trait and not the result of some kind of "maternal deprivation", at that point in time at any rate, I was delighted for my brother in our having jointly "discovered" the earliest known photograph of himself at less than one month of age! That photograph is set out as Fig 8 below.

Fig 8: Mum holding Baby John (on his Christening day, 31 May 1954?)

(d) Joanna (and Maas Bab)

But, with one mystery seemingly solved, it seems, we ought now to go on to face another. That is: why was *Joanna* (from among all of my parents' many available relatives in Montserrat) chosen as substitute mother? For lots of other

British Caribbean islanders were doing exactly the same as our parents in the 1950s and 1960s, and the custodian for the left-behind child (or children) was normally the maternal grandmother. In the case of David and John, however, it just so happened that their mother's own mother - that is to say, Margaret's mother Mary - had already gone overseas for the betterment of her own economic prospects. For Mary had, in fact, beaten her daughter in the race - or the fashion of the time - to emigrate overseas in order to seek superior employment and, thus, secure a much improved standard of living.

Since first writing the above passage, I have travelled (in June 2008) to the eastern England town of Ipswich in the county of Suffolk in order to visit the grave of my mother's mother, Mary. This is because she had died in that town in the winter of 1993. But after paying my due respects to my maternal grandmother at the town's main cemetery, I also took the opportunity to pay a visit to a lady named Charlotte and her husband, Joe Richardson – a couple who now live in Ipswich but who also originally came from my native Montserrat. During her life, my mother had often described Charlotte to me as having been a very close "friend" during their girlhoods "back home". Upon meeting Charlotte during my recent visit, however, it became clear that she was a lot more close to my mother than just a "friend" - and that she was, in fact, my Mum's first cousin! This is because they were the children of two siblings – my mother's father, John Carty, and Charlotte's mother, Frances (*née* Carty). Moreover, Charlotte was to tell me, during the visit, that she and my mother were of approximately the same age and had lived in the same "yard" in the St Patrick's Village area of "south" Montserrat "from about the age of 8".

During my Ipswich visit, Charlotte also went on to reveal a fact which solved the "why Joanna?" mystery for me. This new information was that, before coming to live in her father's house (which shared the same backyard as the house of Charlotte's mother), my mother had previously resided with Joanna – her maternal grandmother. According to Charlotte, my mother's mother, Mary, had given birth to my Mum at the age of about 16 or 17 – a co-production fathered by (or featuring in a starring role) Charlotte's uncle, John Carty. And instead of bringing my mother up herself, my grandmother Mary had left her only child (by blood) in the custody and care of Joanna – Mary's own mother – and had gone off to Antigua in order to take up employment there.

Thus, in turning (in 1955) to her own one-time substitute mother (and, incidentally, maternal grandmother), Joanna, and asking Joanna to be (again) a stand-in mum - for her own first-born boys on that second occasion - my mother was merely asking Joanna to: "Let history repeat itself". This time, however, it was to be two potential little tear-away boys instead of one, no doubt, dutiful and obedient little girl!

My mother had been born in Montserrat on the 10th of September 1927. This means that when she emigrated around March 1955 she would have been approaching her 28th birthday. Now, let us take a "worse case" scenario and assume that Joanna had given birth to her daughter, Mary, at the age of 15 and that Mary had also been the teenage mother of my Mum at the same equally precocious age. On such rather extravagant assumptions, it would mean that my great-grandmother Joanna would have been *at least* 58 years of age when my mother emigrated!

Since first writing the foregoing paragraph I have, as stated, visited my grandmother Mary's grave in Ipswich, Suffolk. Her gravestone announces to the world that she had died on the 23rd of December 1993 "aged 82". This means that she had been born in either 1910 or 1911. Since her daughter, my mother Margaret, was born in 1927, this would mean that in fact she (Mary) would have been 16 or 17 years old when Margaret had been born. We can thus add about two years to my initial estimation of how old Joanna would have been – at her youngest probable age – when she took over custody of us boys from our mother in 1955. This would, therefore, make Joanna about 60 years of age - at least!

Since writing even the "updated" last paragraph above in 2008, I have travelled even further afield from my present base of East Anglia in search of my roots. Indeed, on the 23rd and 24th of February 2010, I revisited my native Emerald Isle of Montserrat for the first time in nearly a quarter of a century! Whilst there, I was fortunate enough to obtain from the island's Registrar's Office – and, in particular, from a lovely lady member of staff therein named "Sedrica" – the death certificate of my great-grandmother, Joanna Brumble, which I set out below in Fig 9. This, among other things, evidences the facts that she died, aged 86, on the 14th of March 1978. This means that in March 1955, perhaps exactly 23 years beforehand to the very day, when my mother was leaving my brother John and myself in Joanna's custody (prior to setting sail to rejoin her husband, our father, in England) our mother's grandmother would have been some _63_ years of age! For good, sound, management reasons, "Nature" has a way of normally preventing women from conceiving babies from about the age of 50 years old or even earlier. How "unnatural", therefore, must it have been for my great-grandmother to have "acquired" not one but, in effect, two new "babies" when she had already reached an age of some 13 years, or so, beyond her time of normal childbearing?!

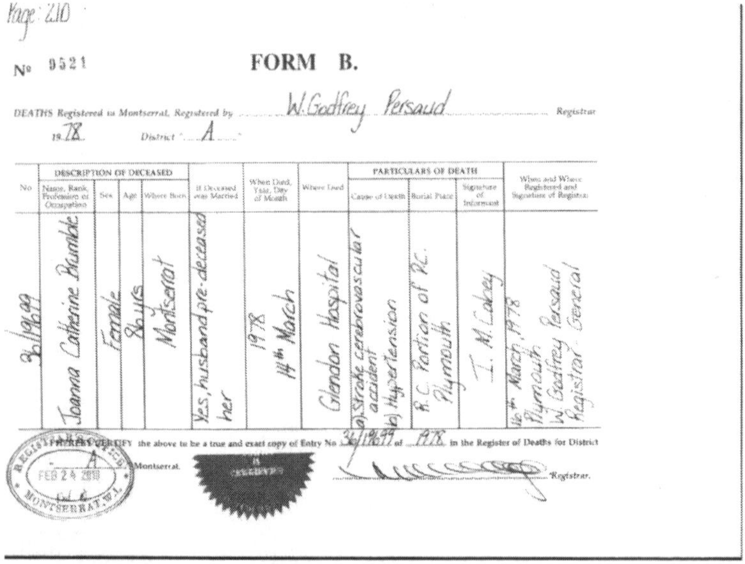

Page: 210

No 9521 FORM B.

DEATHS Registered in Montserrat, Registered by W. Godfrey Persaud Registrar

19 78 District A

No	Name, Rank, Profession or Occupation	Sex	Age	Where Born	If Deceased was Married	When Died, Year, Day of Month	Where Died	Cause of Death	Burial Place	Signature of Informant	When and Where Registered and Signature of Registrar
36/19699	Joanna Catherine Bramble	Female	86 yrs	Montserrat	Yes, husband pre-deceased her	1978 14th March	Glendon Hospital	a) Stroke cerebrovascular accident b) Hypertension	R.C. Portion of P.C. Plymouth	I. M. Cabey	16th March, 1978 Plymouth W. Godfrey Persaud Registrar General

I HEREBY CERTIFY the above to be a true and exact copy of Entry No 36/19699 of 1978 in the Register of Deaths for District A Montserrat.

Registrar.

Fig 9: Copy of the death certificate of the author's great-grandmother, Joanna – showing, among other things, that she died (a widow) in March 1978 aged 86 years

Let us now, therefore, take a closer look at that venerable great-grandmother of mine who, in or about March 1955, was about to take on the not-inconsiderable task of raising two of her great-grandchildren at that "evening" time of her life. A lady whom, I seem to recall, was referred to as "Miss Joanna" by her neighbours, but whom John and I simply (if incorrectly) called our "Granny".

At the time of commencing this book, I did not know if Joanna was ever legally married. I had rather thought otherwise, I will frankly admit. However, throughout the years in which I can remember being in her care in Montserrat she was living with a male partner. His name was pronounced "Maas Bab", which I can only think is the Montserratian version of "Master Bob". So his proper name was probably the formal "Robert" - but it seems to me that "Maas Bab" sounds so much better, and so much more suitable to give the local Caribbean colour which I am seeking to convey in these recollections. I also did not know, on starting this volume, whether Joanna and Maas Bab had any children *together*, but by March 1955 Joanna was the mother of (and, presumably, had previously raised herself) several children of her own. There was, of course, my grandmother Mary. I am pretty sure, from written evidence which I will refer to later in this volume, that Mary's maiden surname was "Greenaway". There was also "Auntie Queen" - who was in fact *my mother's* aunt (but in relation to whom I will refer to by the name which my mother was entitled to call her, rather than the more correct title of "great aunt").

Joanna also had a son. He was one Ben Aymer - my mother's "Uncle Ben", as John and I were also to call him, from the time we first met him in England - a tall (and "great" in other ways) man who was to play a major part in my life, and more particularly in my brother's, in the years to come. He was, indeed, my brother's Godfather – as can be seen from my father's Bible entry in Fig 7 above. Joanna was also the mother of my Mum's "Auntie Esther" - whom I was also to later meet, for the first time, in England and then get to know as the closest "sister-figure" to my Mum in both relationship and age. There had also been another son of Joanna, also called John, whose memory Joanna used to refer us to when trying to stop us two boys from biting our nails.

For her own son, John, had evidently died at a young age, of about 20 or 21, from some illness contracted through his nail-biting - a death which had occurred before we ever came to live with her. Joanna would often tell us - and my nail-biting brother in particular - that she did not want the same fate to befall either one of us little boy charges of hers. There was also yet one more son, whom she referred to as "Phillip" - but I do not recall ever meeting him or know what became of him.

Since writing the foregoing passages about Great-grandma Joanna, her "partner" Maas Bab and the children of Joanna, I have been fortunate enough to meet, in April 2008, with Uncle Ben's half-brother - Mr John White - and his wife, Sarah, at their home in Westbourne Park, London. John (whom I shall refer to by the courtesy title of "Uncle", despite the fact that although he had the same father as Uncle Ben, namely one Daniel Joseph White, "Uncle" John's mother was not Joanna) knew Joanna and Maas Bab well during John's pre-emigration days in Montserrat - even before the couple moved to their new home in Amersham where my brother and I were raised. "Uncle" John surprised me by revealing that, in fact, Joanna and Maas Bab had properly, and legally, been man and wife! Moreover, that Joanna's maiden surname had been "Aymer" prior to her marriage to Maas Bab - which is why Uncle Ben had possessed that particular surname (since he had been born illegitimate to Joanna). And, furthermore, that Auntie Esther had been born legitimate as "Esther Brumble" - thus taking *Maas Bab's* surname.

"Uncle" John was also able to confirm to me that Joanna's own son, John, had indeed died young, in his early twenties. He revealed that, during that deceased son's life, he had been a "leading" steel band player (along with Uncle Ben!) in a Kinsale-based group called the "Blue Skies". Like me, however, "Uncle" John knew very little about Joanna's other son, Phillip - save that he was able to confirm that that other son really existed and that Phillip had been a seaman (who might well have eventually emigrated to the then-colony of British Guiana on the South American mainland (which subsequently became today's independent Republic of Guyana)).

Whilst my grandmother Mary and Auntie Queen probably had the same father[3] - since, to me at any rate, they looked quite similar in their faces - I think it likely that Uncle Ben and Auntie Esther had different sires (given the dissimilarity of the latter two siblings from the former two sisters). Indeed, from the spoken "evidence" of "Uncle" John, the last two children of Joanna, my mother's Uncle Ben and Auntie Esther, also had different fathers (and, thus, different

---

[3] Auntie Queen's maiden name was, more than likely, the same as that of my maternal grandmother, Mary – namely "Greenaway". This assumption arises from the fact that Auntie Queen had a son - an "illegitimate" one? - who possesses that particular surname to this very day. That son is a person whom John and I simply knew as "Clem" during our childhood days in Montserrat. But many, many, years later I was to discover that Clem's "proper name" was, in fact, "Clayton Greenaway". As Joanna's grandson, he used to come and go (abroad to work overseas?), albeit infrequently, during John's and my time in the Brumble household – and, during those times when he was "at home" with us, was a kind of elder brother to John and myself (as opposed to the first cousin, once removed, that he in fact was in our formal family relationship). For Clem was somewhat older than we were – and, perhaps even, in his mid to late teens during the period in question . From time to time, he who would bring back "exotic things" from his travels – such as a brand new, and very small, transistor radio which ran on batteries and with a long, extendable, aerial, with which we could "pick up" Radio Montserrat or Radio Antilles (especially in the evenings, just outside our chattel home). Cousin Clem resides today, with his wife, children and grandchildren, in St Thomas , US Virgin Islands, in the Eastern Caribbean.

surnames) and, to me at any rate, those two children certainly looked unalike between themselves. Of course, in the society of Montserrat in the 1950s – and, most likely, throughout the British Caribbean islands at that time, as well as before and since - it was very common for a woman to have several children by different fathers and so Joanna would not have been out of step with the society in which she then lived. But the significant point being made here is that, by March 1955, Joanna had probably already raised at least six children of her own. The prospect, therefore, of taking on two more "babies", of 30 and 10 months of age respectively, could not have been very attractive for her (or for her husband, who, after all, had no blood relationship with those children). And even if, contrarily, she might have been enthusiastic about the prospective challenge, her energy levels at the age of at least 60 or so would have been unlikely to have been up to the standard needed to provide all the love and full-time nurturing that children of such tender ages would have required in order to flourish in both mind and body.

When I look back to my first memories of my life, therefore, my starting point must be with "my great-grandmother who parented me" - along with her husband Maas Bab. But what was she like? I have another photograph in my collection (see Fig 10 below) which shows all four of the Miss Joanna-Maas Bab household together, outside our "chattel home" dressed in our "Sunday best" outfits and in formal pose. I would seem to be about six or seven years of age at the time, which means that John would have been four or five. We boys are each wearing a white shirt, a Scottish tartan-like tie, dark shorts, long grey socks, and sturdy-looking black shoes. In the photograph, Joanna appears to be an extremely serious, no-nonsense, type of person. She is wearing a wide brimmed hat, which seems to add to her stern demeanour. Maas Bab, too, looks very business-like and formal in his suit and tie. The only hint that he may have been a less severe person than Joanna was at the time, is the positioning of his hat - which is set at a slightly jaunty angle on his head. Once more, I am displaying an unsmiling face to the world - in contrast to that of my brother, which is calm, if not also depicting a slightly amused expression perhaps brought on by the photographer and his antics.

Fig 10: "Un-doctored" photo of "the foursome", in the late 1950s/early 1960s Brumble household – with "Miss Joanna" and

"Maas Bab" in the back row, John left front, and David right front

The evidence, from this second photograph, of the character of Joanna being a serious, if not also a severe, lady ties in with my recollection of her from those childhood days. For, as far as I remember, Maas Bab left all the disciplining of John and myself to her. Perhaps, this was because he felt that he had no right to administer any punishment to us boys, since he did not have any blood relationship with us. Thus, to anticipate the discussion of my schooldays in Montserrat a little, I will relate at this point an episode of misbehaviour by me (and John) which, I can still remember clearly to this very day, which led to Joanna having to administer the "rod of correction" to us. This had to do with the route which we were supposed to take on our way home from our school in Plymouth. When John and I were old enough to walk home by ourselves to our little house in Amersham, about one mile or a little more from our school, Joanna gave us strict "orders" that we were to come home by the most direct way. This meant walking away from the coast road to Kinsale, coming inland, going past the front entrance of Government House and, finally, up the hill to our little hamlet of Amersham. But it was about this time that John and I may have already learnt the rudiments of how to swim - if only to how to manage to successfully stay afloat by doing some sort of "dog paddle". We would, perhaps, have been about the ages we had reached when the foursome, family group, photograph just referred to had been taken. I managed to get John (perhaps against his will) to disobey Joanna's orders and walk home with me via the Kinsale coast road in order for us to have a paddle in the sea, which ran alongside, before proceeding on home to Amersham.

When we got home, "Granny" asked us why we were late and whether we had gone into the sea *en route*. Of course, I steadfastly denied having had any kind of "sea bath" that day - and I managed to get my little brother to support me in such denial. However, we were undone when Joanna checked behind our ears and found salty deposits there - which had resulted from the evaporating action of the hot sun on our skins after our briny seawater dip. She then proceeded to scold us - first of all, for disobeying her orders. But she also reprimanded us, even more, for not realising that we could not fool her so easily! Thereafter, she went for her "tammon whip" (that is to say, a flexible twig picked from a tamarind tree) and beat us with it for our double set of sins.

I do not recall, however, the beating - or "lashes", as I seem to remember we referred to such punishment - being particularly severely or brutally administered by our "Granny". At any rate, it did not put me off for long (nor, indeed, my brother, John, who perhaps was given very little choice by me as to which actions of his were necessary to "support" his "big brother") in disobeying the "no sea bath *en route* home" instruction several more times. We took the trouble, however, on those future occasions to make sure that we used the nearby freshwater standpipe on the Kinsale Road beach to wash behind our ears before proceeding home!

Joanna was a regular attendee at the Sunday Mass at St Patrick's Catholic Church in Plymouth. For, like my mother at that time, she was a member of the Roman Church - and, thus, she ensured that John and I were brought up in the same faith. (Indeed, in the light of the revelations made by Mum's cousin Charlotte of Ipswich, referred to earlier, about my mother's early childhood, under Joanna also, it is most likely that my mother had also been a practising Catholic precisely *because of* Joanna!). I suspect that Joanna rather liked dressing up in order to go to the Mass in town on Sundays. And because she wanted us to attend the services with her as well, she made sure that both John and I always had on our "Sunday best" when we accompanied her. This accounts for the few more pictures which I have of John and myself, posing together in smart outfits - and, above all, wearing different pairs of shoes in every one. In one of them (see Fig 11 below), John looks to be about 18 months old, or even more - which means that I must have been just over three years of age (or a little more) at the time. In the picture, I have on a lovely pair of black shoes, with what appears to be large and shiny buckles on the front of them. In another, which is now rather faded (see Fig 12 below) but in which I am about five years to John's three, we have on strikingly white outfits. I recall, though the picture no longer shows this for me, that we each wore the obligatory (for church purposes, at any rate) pair of new shoes. If the shoes were present in each of these photographs, any trace of a smile on my face in any of them is, characteristically, sadly lacking. It is as if my name should, instead, have been "Master Glum" - at least when compared to the countenance of my brother in these photographs, where he appears well-disposed to each photographer and the particular requirements of the likeness-capturing session in question.

Fig 11: From left to right: David with swashbuckling shoes, oversized shorts and hanky in shirt pocket; John in one of his trade mark (even to this day) commemorative tee-shirt, the then-fashionable (one supposes, owing to our Great-grandma's evident sense of fashion) baggy football-style shorts, and a safe-looking pair of lace-up shoes

Fig. 12: David and John making a "whiter than white" appearance. Could it have been David's First Communion Day? If so, where is the "dicky-bow"?

Fig. 13: David standing on the right, exceptionally (or, oddly - very oddly), as we look. Alas, although his face is now damaged in the photograph, the author certainly recalls it being the normal "glum" when it was still wholly visible

It might be thought strange that I should lay such stress on my wearing shoes in each of the photographs in question. The fact is that John and I <u>never</u> wore shoes, except for going to church! The only other exceptional case, of course, was the rare occasion when the photographer came a calling. I can vaguely recall at least one of these occasions. Perhaps, it was that which led to the foursome photograph previously mentioned. But I remember the man with his box camera on a pedestal getting us into position for the shot, or shots, outside in our garden near some bushes or small trees - pomegranate ones, if my memory serves me correctly. I do not, however, recall any flash gun or other explosive device being introduced into the proceedings - as one sees in old Hollywood movies from the 1950s or earlier. This is, perhaps, not surprising given that we would have been operating outside in what was probably the usual bright Caribbean sunshine. Moreover, surely even a glum, but observant, boy would have remembered something as dramatic as a photographer's pyrotechnics by the age of six or seven - which approximate age I would seem to have reached by the time that the foursome, family group, photograph had been taken.

Perhaps, it was whenever the photographer was coming that Joanna used to take us to the Bata shoe shop in Plymouth to get us some new footwear. For if he only came once a year, at the most, our feet would most probably have grown a size or two since the last photograph. And, surely, it would never have done to have sent, to our parents in England, the latest photo of their growing boys without the necessary footwear included in their attire. I can vaguely remember the excitement of going into Bata's and being made a fuss of by the shop assistants. This would include the measuring of our feet and the trying on of various styles. The leathery smell of new shoes, therefore, is a pleasant one for me and takes me straight back to those footwear-fitting days in, possibly, the only specialist shoe shop in 1950s Plymouth.

No doubt Joanna always had the last word - and probably the first - on which particular pair of new shoes John and I would respectively leave the shop with. However, to suggest that she was always a stern and totally forbidding person would be to do her a grave injustice. For I seem to remember her being also prone to loud outbursts of laughter - like most Caribbean peoples in this respect. And though I cannot now recall anything I did in particular which made her laugh, I do possess a photograph of her in which she is smiling - if not positively cackling with mirth (see Fig 14 below).

Fig. 14: Joanna alone - smiling. Or, perhaps, even having a cackle with, or at, the photographer!

I am pretty sure also that Great-grandma Joanna had a liking for a tot of rum on evenings and, unless I am grossly mistaken, may also have relaxed by smoking a clay pipe from time to time. However, what is perhaps crucial to my later emotional development is the fact that I cannot recall ever being embraced or hugged by either Joanna or Maas Bab during my conscious childhood years with them - or being told by them that they loved me. This is not to say that these things did not happen. It is only to say that I do not remember them occurring. Moreover, if such things did not occur, it would not be at all surprising that a venerable lady (and her husband) of about 60 years or more by this time, who had exhausted herself with child-rearing of her own six or more children (as well as my own mother when a girl up to the age of about eight years old), may not have had any reserves left of the natural energy required to give the kinds of expressions of affection which a child needs for an ideal emotional development.

But if Joanna did not demonstrate her love for me in any memorable tactile or verbal manner, she surely did so in her own different ways. For not only did she warn me off (along with John) from the dangerous pursuit of venturing into the sea unaccompanied by an adult, she was also mindful of a particular personal defect which she noticed about my child developmental process and tried to correct (in her own loving way). This problem was one concerning the way I spoke. I had developed a speech defect which, looking back now, was probably some kind of lisp. I suppose this must have been noticed by my great-grandmother around the time that I started school. Joanna, in her love and concern for me, decided to give me her own "home cure". Such a name for her remedy is most apposite, for it involved the use of bacon - probably that "home cured" from the pork of one of the pigs which we kept on our farmstead - for "waste disposal" of left-over foodstuffs and subsequent eating (that is to say, as an example of recycling - 1950s style). In her treatment of me - and I now wonder how many of her own children or grandchildren she had treated similarly in order to acquire

her expertise in correcting the family "lispers" - she placed a
piece of fried bacon on my tongue, or perhaps underneath it,
and left it there for some time. I can no longer remember
how long I had to keep the bacon *in situ,* but I can imagine
that the temptation to eat the deliciously smelling thing must
have been overwhelming for a small, often hungry, little boy
such as I was at the time. I suspect now that, sometimes, the
temptation "won"! But Joanna's treatment must have cured
my lisp in the short term - for at least it stopped me from
talking, or trying to do so, for the duration that the
sweetmeat was lodged in my mouth. In the longer term -
and I also cannot now recall over what period Joanna gave
me her bacon-treatment - my speech defect was cured, for I
have no such condition today. Nor can I recall having one
after first arriving in England. That is not to say that I do not
get tongue-tied even today - but the causes thereof are,
perhaps, unlikely to be connected with any occurrences from
my Montserrat childhood.

I should now like to say something further about Maas Bab -
my first "father-figure" person whom I can consciously
recall. As stated, he was not the disciplinarian in our little
family unit. Rather, I remember him largely as the person
who made the small farmstead, on which we lived, tick. Best
of all, I remember him involving us boys in his farming
activities from an early age. Thus, for example, he would
allow us to help with the animals. From my recollections, we
seem to have had, at least, one or two of nearly every sort of
domestic creature. There were certainly lots of chickens, so
we were able to help with the daily egg collecting. There was
usually at least one cow with a calf, so we could watch
milking in progress and perhaps be allowed to have brief
attempts at "pulling pints" (or, rather, "teats") ourselves. As

alluded to earlier, we also kept a few pigs - totally black ones - on our farm. As a result of those pigs which I first knew as a child, I can still remember how shocked I was at, later on, seeing pink versions of that species in England for the first time. I seem to recall wondering what made them look so anaemic or otherwise unwell.

Unforgettably for me, however, was the fact that, though we had no horses, we always kept a donkey as our beast of burden. It must have been a female one. For I have good reason for remembering trying, on one occasion, to do what Maas Bab had allowed me to do with one or two of his cows in the past. The jenny definitely did not appreciate my attempting to milk it, however, and - for my impudence and, possibly, also my cold fingers - gave me a sudden and very forceful kick with one of its hind legs. The kick caught me full square in my small stomach! Needless to say, I learnt a hard lesson that day and have never revisited - or ever wanted to revisit, unlike the poor convict in ex-Magistrate Eric Crowther's story told at the beginning of this chapter - the area around the back legs of any donkey since!

Above all for me, however, was the fact that Maas Bab kept a small flock of sheep - perhaps no more than six to ten at a time. And, just like my namesake in the Bible, Maas Bab gave this little David the job of being a shepherd to his flock. It was thus my responsibility to herd them up the, then sleeping, volcanic hills from Amersham to their pasture every day before school and to bring them home again at the end of each day. I loved this role and took special pride in this pastoral occupation. I was always especially pleased whenever one of the ewes gave birth to a new set of lambs - feeling as though my good care of "my" flock had in some way been responsible for the new arrivals.

We also had a dog. I seem to recall that we called him "Blackie" because of the colour of his coat. Unfortunately, he did not get on with one of the roosters in our chicken stock. One day Blackie must have ventured too close for the rooster's comfort. You would think that in a battle between a dog and a smaller-in-stature male chicken, the dog would always emerge the winner. However, this was not the result in the case of our Blackie. For, on the occasion in question, the rooster pecked him in the eye and blinded him! I can still remember looking into his face in the days and months following and always seeing a white-blue orb in the eye socket where his second good eye used to be. I also seem to recall that, despite his permanent disability, he was an otherwise active hound after his "mishap". No doubt, however, in his future dealings on our farmstead he gave our chickens (especially the males of that species) as wide a berth as I gave to the hind legs of our female donkey!

Maas Bab also engaged himself in "working the ground" of our farmstead. Thus, I remember well his cultivating several fields of cotton. He used to allow (or, perhaps, "require" as we became older) John and myself to help him pick the fluffy "bolls" of that crop from their clamp-like buds on the bush. We would put what we picked into "cro-kus bags" - which were largish white sacks made of canvas - so that the cotton, with seeds included, could be taken to the "ginnery" in Plymouth for processing. I remember not liking the cotton-picking task very much at all, since it was hard work labouring away in the hot Montserrat sun. Much more fun was to be had picking tomatoes - which our farmstead started growing only, perhaps, after John had also started going to school with me. Even now, I remember that this initiative had something to do with the Canadian government and, perhaps, gave the Brumble household better financial rewards than cotton-growing did. But such latter type of harvesting was far more attractive for us two boys because, unlike the case with cotton, you could *eat* some of the juicy red tomatoes to keep cool, "watered" and "fed" as you went along picking - and eat we certainly did!

I also recall Maas Bab taking me up "the mountain" above Amersham on at least two occasions. Much later, in England, I was to learn that "this mountain" which loomed above our farmstead is in fact called "Chances Peak" – at that, pre-Volcano, time still indisputably Montserrat's highest point, into which an American passenger airline (*en route* to the nearby island of Antigua) was to crash years later. Later still, I was to learn that the range of hills, of which Chances Peak forms a part, is known as the "Soufriere Hills" – and that it is out of that upland range, immediately above where we lived, that the Volcano was to first erupt on 18 July 1995 and which has not ceased erupting up to the time of writing, some 15 years later!

 The first trip up towards the summit of our mountain was in order for me to help him cut down some tree branches and light a fire with them, in a pit. After that, we had to cover the burning embers with soil and leave the resulting smoking dome alone until the next day. I remember that when we returned and uncovered the mound, the embers had miraculously (it seemed to me at the time) turned into small pieces of black charcoal. My task then was to help Maas Bab gather up this charcoal and load the resulting sacks of it onto our donkey - with me keeping well away from its rear end in the process - and then take it back down the mountain to Great-grandma Joanna. For it was with this fuel that she cooked our meals daily - outside the back entrance of our little chattel house, often using her big black metal cooking pot on top of the lit charcoal in her culinary processes.

Maas Bab must also have taught me how to use some of the tools which were instrumental to his work in the fields of our farmstead. One of those which I remember well is the hoe. For once he had come on board the (perhaps Canadian government funded) initiative of growing tomatoes in several of our fields, one of the small jobs which he got me (and perhaps John also) to help him with involved baby tomato plants. I seem to remember that we called these "slips" and that they were probably obtained already propagated from the funding agency in question. They were planted in long rows in the fields, in the middle of small mounds of soil. It was my task to help Maas Bab, from time to time, to hoe between these rows and mounds in order to turn over the soil and rid the little plantation of any weeds and, perhaps, unwanted slugs and the like.

But there is one farmstead tool which I also used and which I shall not be allowed to forget utilising as long as I live. This was the dreaded, sharp, and sickle-shaped implement which we called the "grass-cutter", according to my Uncle Hammy, but simply the "sickle" according to his elder brother Willy. (I shall, thus, use both terms interchangeably in order to keep both of my Dad's brothers happy). Maas Bab must have shown me how to use a sickle in order to cut grass and other greenery for feeding the sheep in my care and also, perhaps, other animals at our farmstead such as our cows, goats and that unforgettable donkey. One day, however, I happened to be in one of our fields some distance from our chattel house and in possession of a grass-cutter. Whilst swinging the tool around - presumably in the act of earnestly cutting some fodder for some of our animals, as opposed to merely playing with it - I managed to chop it into the instep of my left foot. On deeper reflection, what I now recall (in more detail) actually happened was that, whilst bending forwards, I had gathered together a bundle of grass by their stems, in my right hand, ready for cutting it at the base of the bundle. I had held the sickle in my left hand - for as well as being "legitimate" and "male" as recorded on my birth certificate, I was also born left-handed! In swinging at the clump of grass so held, in my southpaw fashion, I must have missed my target. The sickle thus carried on past the target and came to an abrupt stop some inches into the instep of my left foot - upon which I was balancing in order to perform my inexpert harvesting operation.

The cut was a deep one. It was also wide - perhaps three inches or more across my foot. At first, I could look into the gaping wound and see not only pink exposed inner flesh but also some blue of some of my veins or arteries and some white sinew, ligament or tendon. Very soon, however, these inner views must have been obscured by the out-rushing loss of my blood from the wound. Knowing how I feel about the sight of blood even today, and given the shock of so unexpectedly cutting and causing pain to myself, I have no doubt that I must soon have been close to passing out. Certainly, there would have been no question of my being able to walk home, casually or otherwise, and then explain slowly and coherently to Joanna and Maas Bab just what had happened.

Strangely, for once I cannot remember whether my brother John was with me on that particular occasion when I nearly sliced off my own left foot. I rather think that I had gone out fodder-gathering by myself. However, if I was alone on the ground when the accident occurred, my guardian angel must have been watching over me from the heavens that day. For along came a man - a stranger to me, I think - who must have seen the seriousness of the situation fairly quickly. For, instead of taking me home to Joanna and Maas Bab in order for them to decide what was to be done with me, he made his "executive decision" to pick me up and carry me all the way to the hospital in Plymouth. It must have been over one mile that he walked with me to town and it could not have been an easy one, across several fields and with a heavy-ish small boy of perhaps six, seven or eight years by this time – who, very likely, would have been howling from the pain caused by his wound as well and feeling very sorry for himself. At the hospital, I can remember receiving stitches to sew up my gaping wound - not the last such repair job that I would receive on my body during the rest of my youth. Surprisingly, to me today, from this distance in time to that accident, I was not kept in hospital overnight. The incident had occurred in the evening as I recall, and I was allowed to go home after being stitched up. However, even now I can still alarm myself with the thought that but for my "Good Samaritan" - who had come to my rescue, out of the blue - I may well have bled to death in Joanna and Maas Bab's field. At any rate, up to this day I still have a two to three inch prominent scar on the instep of my left foot - which daily serves to remind me of my "brush with death". If only, indeed, I had simply been using a "brush" instead of that almost lethal, sickle-shaped, grass-cutter (held in my "awkward" left hand, as Great-grandma Joanna might have said, and probably *did* say!) on the day in question, I might well have saved myself (and perhaps also my step-parents) a lot of pain and/or anguish on the particular occasion in question!

There was at least one other occasion when I came into medical distress during my childhood days in Montserrat - a distress, however, which had nothing directly to do with Maas Bab. This arose from my love for one of the fruits which grew in various parts of our farmstead. It was a product from Maas Bab's lands which I adored even more – much, much more - than his ripe, red, tomatoes! This was, and is still, my favourite fruit - the mango. For me, this wonderfully sweet-smelling, and tasting, fruit is truly a food for the gods. The potential difficulty, for the small boy that I was then, however, was how to get at a ripe, or ripening, mango that was high up in its tree - a tree on our land which may well have been planted by Maas Bab. No problem for inventive little David! This was because he simply taught himself how to climb the mango tree in question. After all, this was a far easier task than getting to the top of a *coconut* tree in order to harvest the nuts - which he had seen many of the older boys from his Amersham district do many times by somehow clambering up the smooth, but branch-less and often high, coconut tree trunk. At least the mango tree came with fairly low branches, upon which he could perch and rest himself from time to time as he made his way to the ripe fruit of his heart's desire.

Mango trees, however, often contain something more than branches and fruit - namely, "jackspanners"! These are red-coloured, wasp-like, insects which, in my view, are even more ferocious and protective of their nests than the yellow and black coloured wasp which I was to encounter in England later in life. And, most annoyingly, jackspanners always seemed to make their nests just where there was a bunch of ripening mangoes up in the tree. A little mango-scrumping boy, therefore, goes after his treasure very much at his peril. And, unfortunately, on one of my harvesting attempts, via clambering up the tree in question, I just was not careful enough. I must have touched a nest, or in some other way disturbed it. The result was that very, very soon afterwards I was surrounded by a red swarm of jackspanners - all taking aim with their stings at my head, eyes, lips, arms and (because I still wore short trousers at the age I then was) other sensitive body parts! There was nothing for it but to let go of the branches supporting me and fall out of the tree, get up, and make a run for it - pursued by that red, and very angry, swarm. Whilst I do not recall having to visit the hospital again on that occasion, I can recall having my eyes "boong up" (as Montserratians say) – that is to say, swollen up, black and blue - for some time afterwards. I had had a set-to with some of the jackspanners of Amersham, had come off second-best, and had acquired the souvenir of a "mash-up" face to prove it.

Chapter 2:
Schooldays in Montserrat

(a) BAREFOOT Boys and our School

I cannot at all remember my first day at school - though I can that of my brother, John, very well indeed. Of John's experience, I will say more later. But I must remind my readers that throughout our school careers in Montserrat we wore no shoes to get to and from our classes! (Indeed, to the best of my recollection, we also wore no school uniform, and had no satchel or backpack for our things). As stated earlier, our shoes were perhaps one of the very best things that we possessed in the world and so they were strictly to be worn only on special occasions - namely, for trips to church and the annual photographer's visits. School was, thus, not "special" enough - so we trod there and back in a shoeless fashion every weekday during each academic year.

In fact, I recall that there was at least a short time during our school careers in Montserrat when John and I used to come home for lunch and return to school for the afternoon session. So we BAREFOOT schoolboys certainly got plenty of practice in walking without shoes, for relatively long distances, during our early childhood. For, it must be remembered, that it was about one mile or more from our home in Amersham to Plymouth and our school was in fact located close to the centre of the capital. If we went home for lunch, this would mean that we walked at least four miles every day - and I think that it was, perhaps, even further than a mile from our farmstead to our classrooms. So, as well as becoming fitter and fitter little chaps with each passing academic year, we were also acquiring ever more toughened feet day by day.

It should not be thought that our great-grandmother Joanna was being cruel or neglectful to us by making us go unshod to school. Far from it, for, as I recall, everyone else in my classes - including the girls - came to school the same way. At any rate, I do not remember feeling different from any one else in the class or, perhaps, feeling that I was the poorest of the poor. In short, I do not recall any feelings of shame at all in coming to school shoeless. For, if I had felt this, I think I might well have remembered this negative emotion all these many years afterwards - just as I *do* remember not liking picking cotton in the hot sun (and which cotton-picking matter I have said something about in the previous chapter).

My school was attached to St Patrick's Roman Catholic Church in Plymouth. Surprisingly, therefore, our nearby place of education was given an entirely different moniker - namely, that of "St Augustine's". It was only a primary school, but it was divided into two parts. The infants' section was on the opposite side of the road to the church - on the right hand side of the road as you come out of the centre of

Plymouth heading in a north-easterly direction. The section for the older children - the juniors - was adjacent to the church, and situated in much larger grounds than its infants' counterpart across the road.

I cannot even recall being taught in any of the classrooms in the infants' section. But I must have spent a year or two in that part of the school - for, as long as I live, I will never forget the toilets that we had to use there! They were outside ones - and were "the pits", or, rather, "above the pits", literally. Set up in a block of, I suppose, four or five units, they were situated away from the classrooms on the other side of the grassy playing area. These "WCs" were ghastly. This was because they were not water closets at all - since no water was involved in their "operation". Rather, they consisted of deep holes in the ground, above which platforms for sitting on were constructed - with small holes, in the top of each, suitable for accommodating a child's bottom. Owing to the absence of a flushing system, the deposits from the pupils merely accumulated a few feet below the platforms and the result was an almighty stink if you ever ventured anywhere near the toilet block. Worse still was to be experienced if you actually had to use it! For, apart from the all-pervading smell, there was the fact that you could actually look into each hole and see how the deposits below were building up. Being curious children, many of us (or at least little David, whilst squeezing tightly his rather large and, it would seem, over-sensitive nose) did so look. The memory of having done so, at least once, stays with me to this very day.

Reflecting hard on my stay in the infants' section of my school, one other memory came back to me during the night recently. This is the fact that, in this first school section, one had to make sufficient progress in class in order to graduate or progress to the next higher class. If you did not make such progress, you had to "stay back". This meant that there were boys and girls in my class who were older than me - since they had been held back from advancing with their peers for one or more school years before I had first arrived in their class. I cannot now remember whether "adequate progress" was tested by formal exams in, say, reading, writing and arithmetic. However, I must have made such progress for I cannot recall being ever held back from "going up" to the next class - and I certainly, eventually, advanced to the junior section across the road.

(b) Early crime!

I must also have learned how to read without too much problem, for I certainly recall acquiring a liking for books from as far back as I can remember. Of course, I (or, rather, Joanna) was not in any sort of position to be able to buy picture books for myself just because I liked them and desired to have one (or more) of my own. Nor can I recollect ever joining a library. Perhaps, there was only one available on the entire island at the time - in the capital, Plymouth, I would suppose - but I certainly do not remember ever visiting it.

Of course, my lack of any funding to buy books, and my ignorance of the existence and function of a public library in my neighbourhood, did not stop me from in fact "acquiring" at least one big picture book of my own. For I simply stole it from the garden of one of my Amersham neighbours whose family lived a few hundred yards down the hill from me.

Thus, I began my involvement with the criminal law at the early age of about five years old!

Perhaps, therefore, Alice Miller - from whose 1995 book, *"The Drama of Being a Child"*, we quoted in Chapter 1 above - was not wrong in theorising that traumatic shocks in childhood (and, surely, suddenly losing one's mother would qualify here) *"is the root cause of [among other things]…criminality"*[4].

The pilfered article was a large book of fairy tales containing stories, accompanied by multicoloured illustrations, such as Hansel and Gretel, Goldilocks and the Three Bears, Rumpelstiltskin, and Little Red Riding Hood. I must have spied the book, from time to time, lying about with others in the neighbours' yard as John and myself BAREFOOTed our way to and from school each day. I seem to recall that those neighbours lived in a "proper" (that is to say, non-chattel) house and that they were either a white family or, what we called in Montserrat at the time, "red". Red, in this context, meant being of a brownish colour (a hue also referred to as being "fair-skinned") - with, perhaps, less-tightly curled hair than John and I possessed. Such "redness" would have been the consequence of a mating between a white man (or woman - in theory - though I knew of no examples of this during my life in Montserrat) and their black (that is to say, Negro) counterpart. Such "red" folk of adult age would normally hold better jobs than their pure Negro fellow-islanders - jobs such as teachers, bank clerks and the like. Thus, the child or children from the family of my neighbours in question would likely have had a very good chance of acquiring (in a non-criminal fashion) nicely

---

[4] See footnote 2 above, and the text relating thereto.

illustrated picture books bought for them by their, probably, comfortably-off father or mother. Certainly, if I felt any pangs of my Roman Catholic conscience arising from my theft of the book, these did not last too long. For, having acquired the volume in question, I then kept it in my possession for as long as I remained on the island afterwards.

That book of tall tales, which probably also included a picture of the "Giant" in Jack and the Beanstalk, was almost certainly one of the major influences in the intellectual development of little David. For it not only introduced me, via a really tall tree, to the upper realms inhabited by such gargantuan people, but it also opened my mind to the world, right here on earth, of fairies, wicked witches, ogres, princesses, castles, talking bears, big bad wolves and the like. In short, the volume stimulated and nurtured my nascent imagination to an extent which it is difficult to underplay - even these 50 years on from the act of larceny by which I had acquired it. Reading the fairy tales contained within the tome also developed my vocabulary in relation to new words which I was unlikely to ever hear spoken within the relatively limited Montserratian social life and milieu which I was experiencing at the time. For example, in reading aloud the stories, I can still remember that I came across the longish word - for a young and diffident reader anyway - "cupboard". Until I came to England, I would read this word aloud as per the two separate words of, first, "cup" and then, "board - since in Montserrat, in the 1950s, we referred to such item of furniture as a "dresser" or "press". Moreover, there was no one "schooled", or well-travelled, enough who was present with me, whenever I was haltingly declaiming from my stolen book, who could teach me that the locals in England would pronounce the longer word used in the book in a peculiar way compared to how the word appears on the page - that is to say, as: "cub-bud"!

(c) Into the Juniors (and the private school)

Much more vivid for me are my memories of my Montserrat schooldays *after* I had transferred from the infants' to the school's "senior" - or rather the "junior proper" - section across the road. For although (surprisingly, in view of my recollections of the "crappers" in the first school's playground) I cannot remember, at all, any toilet block in that new section of the school, I can distinctly recall actually sitting in a classroom there and learning from a teacher. Alas, my memory has now faded in relation to any of the teachers who actually taught me in that class - either in particular, or in that section of the school in general. Neither can I now remember any of my fellow classmates - except one. A girl! Her name was Theresa Grey, or Gray. Despite her surname, she was in fact more of a "red". For, I recall that she had very light-brown skin. She also had very long hair which she kept tidy by means of tying it into a ponytail which ran down the length of her back. it was that extension of well-coiffured hair which gave me the first feeling, in my then still young life, of being attracted to a member of the opposite sex. Alas, Theresa was not in the least bit interested in me. It is just possible that she was one of the few of those in my class who wore shoes to school. If so, it would not have been surprising if she had felt far too superior to make friends with the likes of an unshod fellow-pupil like me.

In fact, Theresa was perhaps the kind of well-bred little child who might have been better placed in the small private school which was situated across the road - adjacent to the infants' section of my school. That private establishment was located in part of a convent containing Catholic nuns - from Belgium (as I was to learn over a generation later). But, as well as genteel young ladies, that private institution also took in boys. I think, looking back now, that many of the pupils there would probably have been children of Montserrat's expatriate community - including, perhaps, teachers from England.

From my memory, I can only recall ever venturing into the private school once. This was for a school lunch. By the time in question, I was already staying at school for my midday meal. Perhaps, the walk home and back for such a repast was found to be not a very feasible one in the relatively short time allowed. Or, possibly, the tarmac road home was found to be too hot in the middle of the day for our little unshod feet. Whatever the reason, I remember staying-on at my junior school for what was always the <u>same</u> meal. I cannot exactly recollect what that was now, except that it was something unappealing such as cooked breadfruit (only?) or perhaps rice pudding (only?). Or perhaps it was both - the main course and the dessert. Whatever the truth, the fact is that the fare never varied.

It might have been because our own school's cooking facilities had broken down that particular day which required us to use the refectory of the private school. Whatever the reason, I remember receiving, at that "posher" institution, and polishing off, an extremely tasty meal - which no doubt had included some meat or fish. Sadly for us, the kitchen (or other) problems at our own school must have been quickly sorted out. For, after that special, one-off, and surprise school lunch, I was never again to have the privilege of seeing how well "the other half" lived - or, rather, ate - at that neighbouring private educational establishment.

During an earlier period in my Montserrat school life, whilst I was still going home for lunch with my brother John, I remember that sometimes, on the return journey to school, one of the teachers in town used to stop his car (also containing his own son) and give us a lift back to town. I seem to recall that the son was about the same age as me and might well have been called "Neville", which name I shall call him for these purposes. But his father would have been a very rare man in the Amersham community in being able to own a car. This leads me into speculating, now, that perhaps Neville's father was (at the time in question) a teacher at the private school, and that Neville himself may have been a pupil there. Whatever the case, that repeated act of kindness of the father - which he only bestowed on John and myself from time to time, and never on a daily or even regular basis - is a Christian deed which I have never forgotten in all these years.

Neville's father's car was small and black. It was, perhaps, a Morris Minor - though I know very little about cars, particularly vintage ones emanating from the middle to late 1950s. It could also have been the very first car in which I was ever to be transported whilst living in Montserrat - though I well remember travelling in a taxi, with Joanna and my brother, from Plymouth to our home on other, very rare, occasions. One memory from such car journeys in those early days stays with me still - which I have never heard anyone else say that they have ever similarly experienced. This is the feeling, when the car is travelling, that I was perfectly stationary but that the world of trees, buildings etc on both sides of the car were rushing past. I am not sure that

I ever lost this strange, but enjoyable, sensation when travelling by car as a small child – or, at least, not until my Montserrat schooldays were over. But, then, I had not travelled in such relatively "new-fangled" horseless – or should that be "donkey-less", in my case? – carriages more than, perhaps, twenty times by the time that my island educational era ended.

(d) Brother John starts school

As previously mentioned, the private school was situated next door to the publicly-funded infants' section of my own institution. In that last-mentioned primary department, we find my brother John starting his formal educational life about two years after I would have done so. This, therefore, brings us up to about 1959, I suppose, when John would have been about five years old. I remember that first school day of my little brother very well indeed - even after all these years. For, on that occasion, John had definitely decided that he did not like the idea of going to school one little bit. He howled when he was initially taken to his first class and then handed over (by Joanna, who had come to see him "settle in", and with me looking on) to the company of his first teacher and fellow class mates. He bawled and bawled and was inconsolable when we, eventually, had to leave him behind, despite his fractious state.

I expect that, throughout that first morning, he would have had to have been restrained by his teacher in order to prevent him running after, or looking for, his great-grandmother and his big brother. However, Joanna must have known from her previous experiences with her own children's (and, perhaps, even my mother's) respective first school days - and perhaps I had behaved equally "badly" on my own initiation to formal education, or even worse - that John would, in time, settle down to his new life. I am sure that he quickly did. This is because I cannot remember him throwing any more tantrums the next day, or on subsequent days, when we left him in his new learning environment. At any rate, I cannot recall him ever "going missing" nor anything equally memorable or disastrous during those earliest school days of his - such as, for instance, throwing himself into any of those "WCs" in the toilet block situated so very near to his classroom. John's failure to do the last must have come as something of a relief to me at the time. For this is one "big brother" who would definitely not have fancied the grim task of helping to "fish" his dear, cherub-faced, little brother out of that stinking place!

(e) My "starring" roles

It must have been about the time that John was starting school (in, or about, 1959), that I was selected to take part in a school play given by our "junior" section across the road from John's classroom. Most appropriately, I now think, I was given the role of playing the devil! The play included a scene from the Garden of Eden, as told by the Book of Genesis in the Old Testament. For my part, I had to wrap myself around our stage tree. I did not have many lines to learn, as I now recall. But the timing of what I had to say, however, was important to the proper running of the play's presentation. Alas, for both myself and the overall production, I blurted out words along the lines of: "Eve, Eve - taste of this apple", whilst, at the same time, offering the shiny red prop of that fruit to the girl playing the part of Adam's "wife". All would have been well except that I had done so (in my eagerness to put on a good show and, very likely, extreme nervousness), long before my cue had arrived. It could have been in the important scene beforehand where Adam was creating Eve from his rib. But whenever my "premature ejaculation" had occurred, I seem to recall that the teacher directing the play was not very pleased with me for my rashness in "stealing the scene" - or, perhaps, even "murdering" it. For, as far as I remember, I was never asked to appear in any school play again - either in Montserrat or, even later on, anywhere else in the world!

Another example of my over-eagerness, or exuberance, during my school days in my native land also comes to mind. This concerned the occasion of my making my "First Communion" - an important "rite of passage" in a Catholic child's life which he or she will normally prepare for around the age of seven or eight years of age. Certainly, that was about the age that I had reached when I made mine. This would thus bring us to 1959 or 1960. We had already made our "First Confession" during one of the schooldays which immediately preceded the much-anticipated day. Joanna had dressed me up in a white shirt and white shorts, I seem to remember. Above all, she had also acquired a "dicky bow" for me to wear - made of a lovely Scottish tartan pattern. The great day - a Sunday - finally arrived, after all the preparations and rehearsals for the event at school during the preceding week. Moreover, the bishop himself came to officiate in the service in St Patrick's Church - right next door to our junior section of the school, on the same side of the road.

During the service, the bishop - whom I now understand would have had to have come over to Montserrat, specially, from his base in neighbouring Antigua - came close to the pews in which the First Communicants sat. This was, evidently, in order to enable him to address us more informally and intimately. He began by asking us if we were enjoying the service. Some, only, of the group - and there must have been at least 20 or 30 of us - answered under their breaths, but not in unison, that they were so doing. The bishop was clearly not satisfied with such a quiet and disjointed response from his charges and, therefore, said something further to us along the following lines:

> "I am going to ask you that question again, and when I do I want you all to answer me together with a loud 'yes'. So: are you enjoying your First Communion Service?"

Immediately, I answered, *at the top of my voice* - that is to say, with a great shout:

> *"YEAH-ESS!!! "*

My answer would probably have been heard clearly from the front of the church to the very back. Unfortunately for me, I was the <u>only</u> one of the entire group who bothered to follow the bishop's instructions. To this day, I still feel mortified by my action when I think about it - as well as let down by the rest of the group whom I had naively thought would do just the same as I had done, and at the same moment. No doubt the bishop would have been somewhat amused by what had occurred - even if, perhaps, my great-grandmother (sitting with the rest of the general congregation behind the First Communicants) would have been rather embarrassed for me - having to suffer so much "egg on my face" (or "egg pan yo' fierce", as she might well have said it herself) all by myself in that great big church.

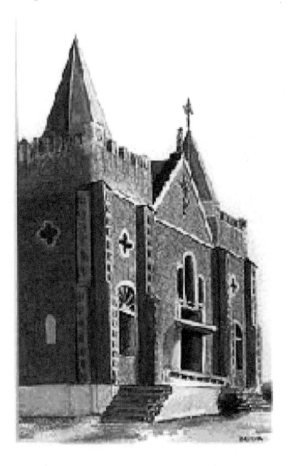

Fig 15: Painting of the front of St Patrick's RC Church, Plymouth, Montserrat - showing the front entrance, as it would have been when the author made his First Communion there in the 1950s

Fig 16: St Patrick's Roman Catholic Church, Plymouth Montserrat – after the relatively recent Soufriere Hills volcanic eruptions (which began in 1995). The author's junior school - St Augustine's RC School - adjoins the church and is, thus, also buried under the volcanic ash to be seen in the photograph. This amazing image is used with the blessing and kind permission of the copyright owner, Dr Richard Roscoe (www.photovolcanica.com)

(f) Death to a schoolboy

With reference to things to do with "rites of passage" generally, there is also something which I can recall from my schooldays which relates to *the* final "passage" - namely death, funerals and the journey to the cemetery for burial. For, right across the road from St Patrick's Church and a little to the left, there was an undertaker's workshop. Perhaps, it would be more accurate to say that it was a carpenter's workshop - in which coffins were also made as part of the services which its owner provided. So if ever I was coming out of the church on a weekday (because, for instance, it was what Catholics call a "Holy Day of Obligation", such as Ash Wednesday, when attendance at a Mass for the pupils of my school was compulsory), or by simply dallying in the roadside opposite the junior section of my school after classes were over for the day, I would have been able to see and hear the hive of activity going on inside the carpenter's workshop. And, at that formative period of my life, the most nervous and curious sensation would engulf me whenever I saw a coffin in the process of being made - a disturbance to my emotional equilibrium which can easily revisit me to this day whenever, for example, I happen to see a hearse passing by bearing its passenger on his or her last journey. Perhaps, the strange sensation in question (which I experienced from my earliest schooldays) arose in me because, in my little mind, to see a coffin being made signalled to me that someone had recently died. And, perhaps, even at the age of five years old or so, it was for me the most serious thing imaginable. For I had, by then, experienced the finality of death among some of the animals on our farmstead. (This had occurred, for example, to one of our cows - "Trudy", as I seem to recall, was her name – when she had fallen into a pit and had died there because Maas Bab did not, himself, have any equipment, or other help which he could call on (or afford to pay for), to enable him to get her out again). So, even at that tender first-school age, my little mind must have been thinking something along the following lines: for a loved farm animal to die was bad enough; but for a human being to have his or her life ended was something many times more serious.

I also knew, at the time of my witnessing the goings-on in the undertaker's workshop, that when someone died arrangements for the funeral would have to be quickly made. This was because of the warm temperatures which Montserrat, along with its neighbouring Caribbean islands, enjoyed. Therefore, a person would often be buried on the same day on which he or she had died, or the very next day at latest. As the brother of my Mum's Uncle Ben - a brother whose name is Mr John White and whom we have already mentioned in Chapter 1 - was to tell me when I interviewed him on Saturday, the 12th of April 2008 in London: "There was no mortuary in Montserrat at that time". Accordingly, (he went on to explain) if an islander died in the morning "you bury them same day"; but if he or she died in the afternoon or evening then "you bury them next day". As a result, "Uncle" John told me that he often witnessed his (and Uncle Ben's) father, Mr Daniel Joseph White - who was, then, not only a shipwright, but also a part-time carpenter – "pulling together" with other neighbouring carpenters (such as Mr Richard Ryan of Kinsale), at very short notice, in order to make a coffin for the burial of some neighbour or other who had passed away that very day or the previous one.

I seem to recall knowing such "facts of life and death" at an early age, but the reality (which I suppose stoked-up my curiosity about human death even further) was that I was never to see a dead person, or even attend a funeral as a mourner, during my boyhood days in Montserrat. I did, however, witness, in person, many a funeral procession passing by - *en route* from one of the several churches in Plymouth, such as our own Catholic one, to the public cemetery out at (or, rather, next-door-to) Bathfield (pronounced "Bart-feel" by Montserratians at the time, I seem to recall). What I also remember about these obsequies was that each procession in question was always preceded by Montserrat's version, at that time, of a hearse. But, this was not a car-like vehicle at all. Rather, it was purely and simply a truck! A truck with an open back – into the well of which the coffin would be transported. The vehicle would be decorated with greenery from palm trees, and plenty of mourners (or perhaps the undertakers) would be "riding (or, rather, standing) shotgun" alongside the coffin. The greater majority of the mourners, however, (usually a long tail of them) would then follow the truck, slowly, on foot. Unlike my understanding of some southern USA funerals (in, say, New Orleans, Louisiana), I cannot recall the Montserratian ones which I witnessed being accompanied by any instrumental music such as that made by a band, whether brass, steel drums, or otherwise - though there may well have been the singing of hymns along, at least, part of the mile or so route from Plymouth to Bathfield.

(g) Outings to netball at Bathfield

Whilst I never was part of any such funeral procession - or ever even mischievously *followed* one (out of the usual human-nature curiosity which I seem to have possessed in great abundance at that time) - to Bathfield, I did venture into the general location of the public cemetery in question on at least a few occasions. These "venturings" were to constitute the further exceptions to my boyhood life in Montserrat of strictly staying within the bounds of my "triangular area of familiarity" (which area, or district, I will deal with in more detail shortly). The exceptional outings in

David R. Bradshaw

question comprised my going to the sports ground at Bathfield, right next to the public cemetery, in order to witness Montserrat playing netball matches against teams from some of the other Caribbean islands. I seem to remember being taken to "watch" Montserrat so competing on at least two separate occasions. And though I can no longer recall which adult, or adults, took me (and also John, perhaps) along to such sporting events, I am pretty sure that it was not Joanna who did so. At any rate, I also recall that I was told at the time that Montserrat had an extremely good team - one that was better than those from the neighbouring islands which had also come to Bathfield for each netball tournament in question.

Alas, on each occasion in question, as there were so many people present (and owing to my, unsurprising, shortage of height at that stage of my life) I was not able to peer over the heads of the adults and taller people in the crowd in order to witness for myself just how good my home-island team was. For Bathfield was not a stadium in any modern sense of that word. There were no raised sides to allow those who were vertically-challenged like myself, or simply further away from the game in question, to be able to see over the top of the taller or more forward spectators. However, I seem to recall, on both my Bathfield visits, experiencing the compensatory feelings of being in the middle of a happy throng of Montserratian people, young and older, who were proud of their "champion" netball team from one of the smallest islands in the British Caribbean. Above all, there was also the great tangible (and "lickable", in its kinder, non-corporal punishment sense) benefit of being treated by my adult escort or escorts, whilst at each tournament, to a rare (for me, at any rate) ice cream which I could devour from my very own cornet!

(h) Childhood recreations

Of course, netball is a game for girls and ladies. The popular male counterpart game in Montserrat, at the time of my Bathfield outings, would almost certainly have been cricket. This is as opposed to football (or "soccer" as some Americans insist in calling the "beautiful game"), which would have been the case in England. Indeed, I seem to recall that Bathfield was also the home ground of Montserrat's "national" cricket team. Alas, despite the popularity in the 1950s of the bat-and-ball game throughout the British Caribbean islands (and on British Guiana, situated on the mainland of South America) - which territories provided players for the ever more successful overall "West Indies" cricket team of the period - I never saw my national island team play in that particular sport. Even worse, whilst living in Montserrat, I never participated in any cricket game myself - either at school, or at home with other boys, say, from my immediate neighbourhood in Amersham. For, in contrast to the position which I was to find out (in years to come) was the norm for schools in England, my school in Montserrat did not organise any games for the pupils (such as cricket and football for the boys, netball for the girls, or swimming lessons for both). Indeed, I cannot remember there being any formal "games", or "PE", periods in the school timetable as such - other than our general "playtimes". And, certainly, even by the stage of the older "junior" section of the school (which I had reached by 1960 or earlier), there was no question of there being organised a "school team" using the best players of, or participants in, any of the suggested sports in order to take on their counterparts from another school in, say, another part of Plymouth (if not elsewhere on the island generally).

But if there was a lack of resource for the organisation of sporting activities for the pupils in my school, during my time there, this did not stop me from devising something of this kind for myself. I have already told (in Chapter 1 above) of the trouble into which I got with Joanna for "swimming" in the sea on the way home from school. I rather think that I should have used the word "paddling" in that earlier context - for I cannot now recall whether "trouble with Joanna" came before or after I had learnt to swim. In fact, however, I never did *properly* learn how to do, say, the front crawl, or the breast stroke, whilst I was still living in Montserrat. However, I used to go at weekends (probably always with John, and also with Joanna's reluctant permission, on such occasions) down the hill from our house to the jetty at Kinsale. (I have referred to "Joanna's reluctant permission", but I wonder now, as I write some 50 years on, whether we brothers, in fact, only told our great-grandmother that we were simply "going out to play", generally – and made sure that we did *not* mention that we were really going "bay-ding", as our intended activity was called). The Kinsale jetty extended perhaps 20 to 30 yards out into the sea from the shore and ended where the lovely clear blue, or greeny-blue, water was deep - much too deep for a little boy of say five or six years to stand up in and not be totally submerged, or worse. But I (probably, also always with my little brother in tow) out of my usual curiosity, would often wander to the end of the jetty to watch the bigger boys jumping and diving into the sea from that vantage point. I seem to recall that some of them also fished with line and bait alone (that is to say, never with a rod) for the marine life below - many varieties of which we could see clearly in the translucent water beneath the jetty's sides and terminus.

One day, one of the bigger boys, whom I used to watch diving in from the jetty, must have decided that it was high time for me to stop being a mere spectator in relation to sea sports. Completely unbeknown to me, he came up from behind and gave me a sudden push which launched me into the air - without the welcome slats of the jetty's walkway below to catch me again. I seem to recall thinking, in the second or so before I came down from my "launching", along the following lines (in suitable Montserratian, juvenile, Catholic and, therefore, non-"f"-word language): "This is it!"; and "I am now on my way to a drowning and watery grave!" (Or, perhaps, it was a more Montserrat-like expletive, such as: *"Ah drown, me ah go drown!"*) Once I hit the water I, of course, panicked – "big time", as they say these days! However, my plucky survival instinct kicked in at once and I began to flail around furiously with my arms. To my absolute surprise - a sensation which I can recall very clearly to this day as I write - I did not sink without a trace! On the contrary, I was staying afloat - a feeling which I immediately liked - and, what is more, I was making progress with my flailing arms. I was in fact "dog-paddling" from the very start of my "baptism" in Kinsale's "deep-sea" water - after the initial panic had subsided. That panic further retreated, after several more seconds had passed from my first taking the plunge - or, rather, my being plunged - when I realised that right behind me in the water was the good swimmer and bigger boy who had pushed me in. He had, evidently, jumped in after me in case I had gotten into trouble during my enforced "dip". Imagine, therefore, how proud of myself I was when he offered to hold me up in the water and I was able to push him away and tell him that I did not need his help. For, thanks to him, I had just found out that I had had the ability to "swim" all along. And so, it quickly dawned on me that, for the rest of my life, I was not going to be a mere spectator "by the sea", or even "standing high and dry on the jetty". That is to say, that, henceforward, I would no longer be merely passive, insofar as activities involving my body and the translucent and warm waters of the Caribbean Sea were concerned.

In addition to "swimming", I can also recall a few other "sports" in which I was to participate - outside the classroom or playground - during my schooldays in Montserrat (at about the same time that I first to learnt how to swim, or at least to stay float successfully, off Kinsale jetty). The first of these involved the kite - an artificial one, as opposed to the bird of prey of that name. First, there was the making of it. Once again, I was (easily) led by one or two of the older boys from my Amersham neighbourhood - for I do not recall being ever able to successfully make a kite by myself (or with my little brother's help alone). The construction began with the kite's "skeleton" or frame. This was simply made of two thin bamboo sticks joined together to form a cross - *a la* that used by the Romans for Christ's crucifix. Then we would cover the frame with some coloured crepe paper. This was comprised of a lightweight material and was usually sold in one of the brighter colours of the rainbow such as red, yellow or orange. We bought the paper from one of the stores in Plymouth - and it could not have cost very much, since we poor boys seem to have been able - without committing any larceny from the neighbours' gardens or otherwise - to acquire lots of it for our kite-making. When it was finished, the kite was four-sided (whether looked at from its front or from behind) - with the top two shorter sides forming the shape of the roof of a house and the bottom longer sides forming the shape of the letter "V".

We then had to make the kite's "tail". I seem to recall that we simply used a length from a ball of string which we also had in our possession - through lawful means, if memory serves me correctly. We called such string "twine". A length of this twine would be used, perhaps of no more than six feet, to which we would then tie pieces of rag, at intervals, along such extension of the kite. The completed tail would then be attached to the bottom of the "V" forming the kite's longer sides. The final bit of the "construction" required our tying the tail onto the body of the kite, at the point where the two pieces of bamboo joined to form the crucifix shape, with the rest of the twine remaining as part of the original ball. Then it was time to "launch" the bird and try to get it to fly. I am pretty sure now that if I was unable to make a kite by myself, I did often play a part in running as fast a possible with the potential flyer, and then letting it go from my (left) hand when I was up to full speed. I must have succeeded at least some of the time, for I cannot recall (these 50 years on) being "depressed" about my inability to get any kite, with which I was involved, to fly. I can only recall engaging in such activity with alacrity - which suggests to me that I must have been quite successful at it, for I would not have persisted in following one failure after another for very long. Once the kite was successfully aloft, then the fun could really begin. For, by pulling on the string in certain ways, we boys would be able to make the kite "dance", this way and that, in the air. I would also be able to feel the sensation of the kite pulling on the twine in my hand, which I very much liked because of the strength of the tug on my little, and then not very strong, limb. I seem to recall that we held on to the ball of twine by means of a small piece of wood. We could turn this one way in order to let more twine out to allow the kite to go higher still, or turn it the opposite way to rewind and, thereby, bring the flyer back in and eventually down to earth into our possession again.

But if I was somewhat successful at kite flying, this was not the case with the other "home-made" activity, or "sport", in which I also engaged for a while at the early period in question of my life. This involved the "spinning top" - or "tap", as I suspect we would have pronounced the second word of the toy's name in my Amersham neighbourhood at the time. Again, this activity would first have necessitated the making of the relevant device - mainly by us boys alone. I seem to recall that, for this purpose, you would needed a block of wood of approximately the right shape and size. One of the bigger boys - or perhaps his father - would then have had to have chiselled, and/or sawed, the block into a sort of turnip shape. This, therefore, explains why I would not have liked this spinning top activity very much – for, after my accident with the sickle-like "grass-cutter" in my left hand (during the relatively simple task of harvesting one fistful of animal fodder), God only knows what damage I would have done to the rest of my little body if I had tried to fashion a rough piece of timber into the required wooden turnip-shaped object!

Perhaps, as important as the shape of the top, was the bit of nail that protruded from the smaller, bottom, end of it. For it was upon this protrusion that the top was to be spun - or, as was always the case with me as I seem to recall, was *supposed to* spin. I cannot now recollect, at all, how getting that nail in place was achieved. Perhaps, a longish nail was hammered into the bottom end of the top in the usual way, and then the head of the nail was filed off before the remaining metal stalk was further filed until it became pointed. At any rate, once the nail was successfully in place and given its "point", the next stage in the activity required the twisting of some twine around the body of the toy. This had to start from the protruding nail at the bottom and wind itself around the outer surface of the top to somewhere near its - kindly, gentle reader, excuse the pun - top. Then came the *piece de resistance* action: the would-be top-spinner, whilst holding firmly on to the end of the twine at the upper end of the top, would throw the toy to the ground *and at the same time* pull on the twine to make it spin.

The main aim of the spinning top game, perhaps, was to see which of two or more would-be spinners could make their particular object spin the longest. I seem to remember that those bigger boys who were really good at this activity would be able to make their individual tops spin for perhaps a minute or more. Alas, I was destined to remain amongst the "would-be" spinners - for I cannot recall ever succeeding in getting the object to spin fast enough so as to enable it to remain upright for more than a few seconds before falling over in dismal failure on one of its sides. Moreover, it is just possible that I have described the winding of the twine process completely wrongly, by presenting it in an "upside down" fashion. That is to say, that, perhaps more correctly, the winding should start from the upper end of the top and finish at the protruding nail component at the bottom. But the dual action of throwing the top to the ground and simultaneously whipping the twine to make it spin, is a memory which I shall never forget in its correct detail. The fact that I cannot even remember now which way the winding process was supposed to be accomplished, shows that I was not very good at the "sport" in question - or, perhaps, that the reason for my failure at it was because I always did the winding-up the wrong way round! No doubt, however, I did not persevere with such a failing activity, from my point of view, for very long.

(i) "Colonials" celebrating and/or honouring the British Empire

One of the big events of the school year, which I can still well recall from my time in the "big-part" of my school, was the annual "Empire Day" celebrations. I seem to remember that we actually had a school holiday on that anniversary. But we went to school anyway on the day in question, so that we children on Montserrat could receive a really big treat - or, at any rate, those of us attending St Augustine's School, Plymouth. This was the free gift - for every pupil - of a "bun"! That is to say, the item of food that in England is usually called a "bread-roll". However, the bun was only the *outer* part of the treat. This is because it also contained some (to me at the time) delicious, and lovely smelling, pink meat. What was that filling? It could have been just a slice of ham, I suppose. But going back into the depths of my memory, I rather think it was more likely to have been "Spam" - or some other processed meat of a similar kind. At any rate, because we obtained such a delight but once a year, for at least the two last years of my time at St Augustine's, I was more than happy to queue up and receive my free bun -

with that pink *je-ne-sais-quoi*-filling - along with my fellow schoolmates.

More than likely, the gift of the buns to us Montserrat school children was, in constitutional theory, a present from our Queen-Empress back in England - we being just a very tiny section of her colonial subjects in the British Empire spread across the world. And if I never had the chance to witness that great lady's visit to our particular part of her empire, I can certainly remember well the time when one of her close relatives did so - presumably, on behalf of Queen Elizabeth II herself. This was the day of the visit of the Queen's aunt, the "Princess Royal". I have, long after my schooldays in question, discovered that the latter lady was in fact the only sister of the Queen's father, the (then) late George VI. The Princess Royal's visit to our island must have taken place when I was already in the "big" part of my school. However, I can no longer remember whether or not my standing at the Plymouth seafront waiting, and stretching my little neck, to witness that royal princess' arrival and disembarkation was simply a trip "down the road" organised by my school. However, I rather think now that the occasion might well have been a public holiday proclaimed in celebration of the princess' visit and that Joanna had taken me (and, very likely, also my brother John) along to join the crowd waiting to see her. At any rate, I seem to recall that we were to be disappointed in our quest - for Her Royal Highness did not come ashore from her royal yacht or other ship whilst we were waiting in the throng. Perhaps, we had already missed her walkabout, or were simply much too early for that event. Nevertheless, the memory of being surrounded by a large crowd of Union Jack wavers, looking out into Plymouth Harbour beyond the jetty to the royal craft lying at anchor (with her precious passenger on board, presumably), has stayed with me throughout the 50 or so years since.

(j) Masquerade

Another "festivity" on my native island, which I have distinct recollections of, was the annual "Masquerade" - which I can remember witnessing more than once during my Montserrat schooldays. This celebration, however, was definitely not a school-organised event - for I can recall only ever attending it in the company of my great-grandmother, Joanna (and, more than likely, also with my little brother John in attendance). (In fact, I cannot recollect ever doing anything "social" in Plymouth town which involved Maas Bab - whether it was going to church, shopping for shoes, attending the Masquerade or otherwise. This sudden realisation, these 50 years on, causes me to speculate (as I write) on whether, perhaps, Maas Bab did not like the social airing of himself in the town. Curiously, however, I certainly do not remember him as being a shy, retiring, or "shrinking violet", kind of man back at home on his farmstead in Amersham). And being a Joanna-organised outing, this suggests that my school would have been on holiday during the time of the Masquerade. Such a possibility would thus square with my memory of this annual event being "kept up", or celebrated, sometime around Christmas - perhaps shortly before or, more likely, just after and including the New Year festivities.

As its name suggests, Masquerade, as I remember it at any rate, involved a relatively small number of brightly-dressed individuals leading a crowd of people dancing through the streets of Plymouth. Such activity would have been to the accompaniment of music supplied by drummers and fife, or flute, players – who, simultaneously, participated in the street dancing. I cannot now recall if the shinily-dressed (from head to toe) masqueraders were all male or included some women. It would have been difficult for a small boy to assess their gender in any event, for their faces were hidden by stocking masks!

But, for me, the highlight of the visit to see the Masquerade was to find myself situated within sight of "the Bull", whilst being able to cower behind my great-grandmother's skirts in order to hide if he came too close during the processing of the crowd. For the Bull was a terrifying figure for me - as I suppose it would have been for most children in, or near, the throng of onlookers. He - and to me there was no doubt that the Bull was a *man* "dressed up" - had on a mask which totally covered his head. This mask was in the guise of a large bull's head, complete with a pair of long horns on each side. Moreover, he carried a whiplash which he would crack close to some unfortunate adult, child or group of persons who happened to be near him. What was most scary of all, however, was that the Bull would run erratically through the crowd so that I never knew, from moment to moment, whether he would come over in the direction of Joanna and myself at any particular instant during the procession of the crowd. If he did happen to select you as his target person, he would come right up close to your face with his own bull-like one - and I am sure this would make many a child in the crowd (no doubt, including myself) frightened out of their wits and begin to cry in an effort to get the "creature" to go away and turn his attentions to someone else.

(k) A trip "abroad"

During my Montserrat schooldays, if memory serves me right, I only ventured twice outside my immediate neighbourhood - apart from the two Bathfield netball tournament visits which I mentioned earlier. This immediate vicinity - see Fig 5 in Chapter 1 above - was a very small area of, perhaps, one to two square miles at the most. It was comprised of a triangle with Amersham to Plymouth on the first (north) side, Plymouth to Kinsale on the second (west) side, and Kinsale back to Amersham on the third (east) side. Each side was approximately one mile in distance. One of the two experiences of my venturing outside my "comfort zone", or familiar triangle of everyday life, was the visit of my class to the studios of Radio Montserrat - which was then situated in the St Patrick's Village area of south-west Montserrat (as I understand it now), about two to three miles from Plymouth. This adventure was to enable my class to either record a song (or songs) for later broadcast or, perhaps, to make a live broadcast of the same. I seem to remember that the enterprise was a success. I can only think that my teachers must have had some faith in my singing abilities for them to include me in the class choir - despite my dismal failure as an actor which I have written about earlier in this chapter. Or, perhaps, that the visit to Radio Montserrat pre-dated my disastrous, and career-ending, debut into the world of amateur dramatics.

(l) Introducing "Mr P"

The other time in which I can remember going outside my small, and triangular-shaped, "zone of familiarity" district was when a man named Mr P (not the real first initial of his surname) took John and myself for a joyride in his grey Rover motor car. We must have driven for some miles, well outside Plymouth, but I can no longer recall where exactly we went - or, even, in which direction. This event, I seem to recall, took place one Sunday morning after Mass at St Patrick's Church. For Mr P, too, must have been a member of our Catholic congregation. He was much else besides - for he was a white man and (so I am pretty sure he told my brother and I) a magistrate in Plymouth. Thus, like Mr Eric ("He should not have been such an ass") Crowther from London, whom I quoted at the outset of this book, Mr P was probably also an ex-pat magistrate working in Montserrat on a temporary basis at the time. He also happened to live in a very large house - perhaps the largest in the whole of the Amersham community - which was situated on the top of the hill, on the road up from Kinsale back to our home village. It was perhaps on one of those trips home from school in which I (and John, egged on by me) had disobeyed Joanna's instructions not to go into the sea *en route*, that Mr P may have first encountered us. For, in so disobeying my great-grandmother, we boys would have had to walk right past Mr P's house on our way up the hill from the beach on the Kinsale road.

If I can no longer recall with any certainty how we first met Mr P, I can certainly well remember several occasions in which he either expressly invited us, or allowed us, to visit him in his "mansion". For something nefarious happened to me in that house - and, it is likely, to my brother John also, for he was always with me whenever we visited that place. I certainly did not appreciate fully what was being done to me (or us) at the time, being only about six to eight years old at the time - but I seem to recall having a vague feeling, even then, that it was something "wrong". The fact that I (or we) never told Joanna or Maas Bab, or any other soul, suggests to me now that we must have been sworn to secrecy by Mr P about what he had done to me (or us) in his home. Perhaps it is my Catholic conscience, but I have kept my promise not to report all until now. Not even my wife has been told about this terrible episode in my life (and that of my still younger brother, John). In "successfully" burying that part of my boyhood experiences to the deepest recesses of my consciousness these 50 years or so, I have perhaps stumbled on another reason why there may have been many a "down" side to my life's story. I am now ready to consciously recall, and disclose in this volume, that particular episode at this point in my life as part of my long-term self-healing process. For, it seems to me, I am required to confront my childhood traumas in order to obtain such a holistic restoration, for a happier and more fulfilled life in the future. For such a confrontation to finally occur, during the process of writing this book about the early part of my life's history, is just one more example, it seems to me, of the wisdom of the saying: "better late than never!"

So what did happen in that house? I now know - and not merely because I am a qualified lawyer and a practising Christian as I write this today - that what occurred was legally and morally a case (or cases) of child abuse. However, it seemed to me then - as it still does in a way, even these 50 years on as I write this - that Mr P was anything but "abusive" to me or my little brother. This is because he was, perhaps, the "kindest" person that I had come across during my childhood days in Montserrat. Moreover, he gave us access to a "proper" (ie non-chattel) house. It was a huge place, and something akin to that which I would probably have thought of at the time as being rather like visiting the inside of one of those fabulous castles which I had read about in my stolen book of fairy tales mentioned earlier in this chapter. To enter such a mansion was not ordinarily for the likes of little black boys like John and myself. Indeed, apart from our school, St Patrick's Church, the shops in Plymouth town, the hospital where my left foot was stitched up, my doctor's surgery, and the Radio Montserrat premises, I cannot recall ever venturing inside any other "proper" buildings whilst growing up on my native island.

Once inside this ordinarily impossible-to-enter-into citadel that was Mr P's residence, we encountered a "white man" - as opposed to, say, a merely "red" one - at close quarters. This, again, would not have been an ordinary, everyday, experience in our lives – though, perhaps, our parish priest at the church would also have been white, and certainly some of the nuns who taught at our school were from the "white" continent of Europe. Years after the episodes which I am now recounting, my mother was to tell me that I had been baptised by a "Father De Ridder" and my father's family Bible certainly confirms that that particular priest had, indeed, been the minister who had married my parents in 1949 - three years before my Baptism had taken place in September 1952 (see Fig 21 in Chapter 4 below). Thus, if Father De Ridder had still been the incumbent up to the time of my First Communion, then he is likely to have been also a white man - since his name suggests a Dutch or

Belgian origin. And as I was also to discover, many years after becoming a communicant in my church for the first time, Belgium was certainly the country of origin of some of the nuns who taught at our school. At any rate, clearly I did not get to know any white priest at my church well - for I should have remembered him today if I had done so. In Mr P, however, I (and my little brother) had, most unusually, encountered a white man who also wanted to befriend us!

Having ventured inside Mr P's house, I am sure that he would have treated us to food and drink. I seem to recall being introduced to the passion fruit there - a crop of which, I think, grew in his garden near his garage - and being given drinks by Mr P, made from the juice of such fruit. At this distance in time, I can no longer remember what else we would have been given to drink or eat by him. Whatever it was, however, such fare must have been of a vastly superior quality to that which we were used to in our everyday meals with Joanna and Maas Bab - or to the simple and monotonous fare which we received for our daily school lunch. What I can never forget, however, was using Mr P's showers in his big house. For they contained, it seemed to me then, an unlimited supply of warm water - which I seem to remember I very much wanted to stand under for as long as possible.

No doubt, my serious liking of Mr P's warm shower was as a reaction to the cold standpipe wash which Joanna used to force me to endure as I was growing up under her custody and control. That public faucet or tap, was our single source of water for most of the time I was living with Joanna and Maas Bab, and it was situated a little way down the hill from our chattel house, on the other side of the road. It was also clearly intended for the communal use of all the other villagers thereabouts. I well remember my great-grandma forcing me to "stoop down" and then her holding me under the tap in order to prevent my escape whilst she opened the stopper above me so as to allow the cold water to cascade onto my back and run down to the rest of my body below (which lower body Joanna would then set about scrubbing vigorously with, red-coloured, "carbolic soap"). To this very day, I cannot stand the feel of cold water on my back - or, indeed, anywhere else on my body for that matter! But experiencing it upon my back is still the worst torture for me.

Shortly before leaving St Augustine School, Joanna and Maas Bab's financial circumstances must have improved somewhat, for they were able to have their very own (tall) stand pipe/shower installed on our property - just outside the back of their chattel house. As this new amenity on my step-parents' property saw much less use than its communal counterpart down the road, the water in the exposed part of the pipe on the surface leading to the tap itself would often warm up from the heat of the Montserratian sunshine during the day - which would mean a gloriously warm or, at least, tepid beginning to a shower before the colder water, previously stored in the pipe below ground, would begin to flow. When the latter happened, it was, for me once more, a case of "cover your back" or "get out quick!" (hoping to goodness that I was not still covered in a soapy lather - or, dare I say it, "white").

But I digress! I must stop putting off dealing with Mr P's shower as opposed to my step-parent's more recently acquired rural alternative. In so re-focussing on Mr P's bathroom, I am forced to deal with one of the most sensitive parts of my life story. For, unfortunately, as I now see things from an adult's point of view, in encouraging (or at least allowing) my brother and I to use his own, constantly flowing, warm-water shower, Mr P deliberately, it seems to me now, did not just leave us to enjoy our shower alone. On the contrary, he also stripped off and joined us in it! Perhaps it was here that I was to realise the differences between a man's body and a boy's for the first time in my life. For I cannot recall ever seeing any other adult naked during my childhood days in Montserrat - although boys older than John and myself did still swim in the sea at that time, at the Kinsale beach or jetty just down the hill from Amersham, completely naked (as we brothers had never been lucky enough to have been bought a pair of swimming trunks by Joanna for such sea-bathing purposes - especially as she did not want us to be "bade-ing" in the sea without adult supervision in the first place!). Certainly, I had never seen the "erect member" of an adult man - and a white one at that! - until I had first ventured into Mr P's walk-in shower room. It was a sight I was to see on several future occasions there - as well as the whitish, slimy substance which exuded from its end and which I can recall asking Mr P why the same substance did not also escape from my own much smaller equivalent.

Mr P's shower room must also have contained a flushing toilet bowl. For it was upon that bowl that the most serious act of "abuse" occurred. To embark on this course, he would first sit on the bowl in the normal way. He would then invite me to sit on his lap and, thereafter, the illegal act would begin - in a most gentle way. So gentle, in fact, were his actions that no alarm - as far as I can now remember - was caused to me. It was as if he went out of his way to make it seem that what he was doing to me was a perfectly normal, everyday and natural activity - and, in order to achieve this, he had to ensure that absolutely no fearfulness or distress was caused to me by his actions. He must have succeeded in his strategy, for nothing he did to me spooked me (or my brother) sufficiently enough to prevent me from wanting to return on several more occasions, in order to further sample the warm shower and other treats of Mr P's big house. Indeed, so surreptitious must have been his activities in the regard in question that John and I never spoke either to Mr P, *or to each other*, at the time about what Mr P had done to me (and possibly also my little brother). Even worse, perhaps, given the theories expressed by Alice Miller in her book about child sexual abuse and the effect that suppression of the memories thereof has on the later adult (entitled, *"Thou Shalt Not Be Aware: Society's Betrayal of the Child"* (1998))[5], it could not have helped my (or John's) later emotional development that John and I never spoke to each other (or to any one else, as far as I know) about what had occurred in Mr P's shower room - either at the time of the occurrences there, or subsequently (even by the time we had begun to grow into adolescence and, later, adulthood).

In the foreword of the stated 1998 edition of Alice Miller's book, the then-editor of the Journal of Psychohistory and the editor of the book *"The History of Childhood"* (1974)[6], Lloyd de Mause, states (at p.vii):

"The American Psychiatric Association's current diagnostic manual claims pedophilia is only a psychiatric disorder if it bothers the

---

[5] Published by Pluto, London 1998 – translated by Hildegarde and Hunter Hannum from the German *"Du sollst nichts merken"*

[6] The full title of the cited work is: *"The History of Childhood: the untold story of child abuse"*, edited by Lloyd de Mause and published by Psychohistory Press, New York 1974

pedophile; otherwise, having sex with children is healthy. In fact when I gave a speech at a recent A.P.A. Convention showing that the majority of children in history were sexually abused, the audience reacted by wondering if incest isn't after all <u>not</u> really pathological, since so many have done it. Alice's insight into the unconscious causes of this most universal denial of the harm and its cost to society is, unfortunately, still a lonely one today". (Emphases added). Later on in his foreword, de Mause adds (at pp. vii to viii) the following: "...most adults in the past believed that children didn't remember anything that happened to them up until the age of five, so sexual exploitation, beatings and other severe abuse had no real affect on them.... The attitude was that raping children was an adult prerogative.... Alice Miller demonstrates in this book that one of the far reaching harms is the lack of awareness and the denial of crimes".

In her own Preface to the said 1998 edition of her book, Alice Miller writes (at p. xi): *"The commandment that says: 'Thou shalt not be aware of what was done to thee, nor of what thou doest to others' ensures that cruelty suffered in childhood is played down or modified by memory until it becomes unrecognizable".* Earlier, in the counterpart Preface to the original edition of her book, published in 1981, Miller had already written (at p. viii): *"...the original edition of this book is dedicated to Sigmund Freud on the 125th anniversary of his birth. His discoveries of the <u>survival of childhood experiences in the adult unconscious and the phenomenon of repression</u> have influenced my life and my way of thinking".* (Emphasis added). Finally, in the Preface to the Second Edition of her book published in 1990, Miller writes, more optimistically for child abuse victims it would seem, as follows (at p. vii): *"The Swiss therapist J. Konrad Stettbacher has described the therapy he developed.... This therapy can enable many people to approach their childhood step by step and so assimilate the knowledge they had banished. With the knowledge of one's own* *history…blindness is no longer required as a protection from fear.* <u>*Someone who has faced facts need no longer fear reality nor flee from it*</u>*"*. (Emphasis added).

Putting aside academic writings for the moment and returning to the very real world of Mr P, it must be readily admitted that there were other non-sexual (using the word "sexual" from Mr P's viewpoint only, of course) and good things in the big house which were capable of diverting a curious child (such as I must have been at that particular period of my then relatively short life). For, to give but one example, I can remember Mr P having a big radio set - perhaps it was called a "wireless" in those late 1950s/early 1960s Montserrat days - in one of his sitting rooms. He would allow me to switch it on and play with the dials in order to receive broadcasts from all sorts of exotic places named on the front face of the appliance. John and I must have been visiting him on a Saturday afternoon at least once, for I can still remember hearing the football results from England being read out in the usual BBC fashion - and my asking Mr P to explain what the broadcast was all about. It may have been that Mr P was checking his football pools coupon whilst listening to such results broadcast. This was because, for once, he did not wish me to change to a variety of other stations by doing my usual fiddling with the radio's dials. If he had been so doing, then this would just go to show that those who appear incomparably rich and well-off to a poor BAREFOOT schoolboy are not necessarily so from an adult's point of view (even if that adult is "white" and enjoying what must have been the, no doubt, well-paid post of Magistrate on the island).

Perhaps, however, the biggest treat for me, connected with going to Mr P's house, related to an object that was not so much "in" it as "nearby" - in fact, something situated in the garage attached to the house. I refer, of course, to Mr P's Rover motor car. For although I can only ever recall going for one joy-ride in that vehicle - as previously described - I seem to recollect being allowed by Mr P to just sit in the car even whilst it was merely stationary in the garage. Perhaps I liked the smell of its leather interior, or the fact that it also contained a radio - which I could switch on to listen to some music, or other, programme, or simply fiddle with. In addition - like the father of the previously-mentioned, fellow-Plymouth schoolboy, Neville, in that father's much smaller Morris Minor - Mr P, once or twice, stopped to offer my brother and I a lift to Plymouth when, rarely, he happened to pass us on our way there to school or church.

In short, therefore, Mr P was nothing but kindness to my brother and myself - as far as I was concerned at the time, though I now know that the law and the society around him (then, as well as now) would regard some of his activities to us, inside his house, in a totally different light. Perhaps, my little brother and I were simply victims of a highly-skilled "groomer" of children whom he had targeted for his own nefarious activities. However, Mr P came across to me, at the time, as being a totally kind man and, what is more - and in his moral favour - I never saw any other children in the house when we were there with him (or, indeed, at any time when John and I happen to pass the house without stopping). Indeed, I can only remember his ever having one other visitor whilst we were with him in the house. For, once or twice, a white lady friend of his, or perhaps even "girlfriend", would arrive whilst we were there. Certainly, her being a white "maid" or servant to Mr P would have been as unthinkable then as it would be in the Montserrat of

2008. The lady visitor was on the large, or plump, side as I recall, but she certainly never joined in any of Mr P's said illegal activities with us. So, again in Mr P's moral (if not legal) favour, his home was very far from being the "house of horror" that, I now see (with my adult's eyes), it clearly had the potential of being. In thinking along these lines, the names (and sexual and murderous activities) of the late Fred West and his wife, Rosemary, formerly of Gloucestershire, England, come to mind!

Moreover, my redemption and the salvation of my future life's better prospects (and those of my brother, John) – or, at least, the speed of these things – more than likely came about as a *direct* result of my dealings with Mr P. That is to say: Mr P was, most probably, the catalyst for the rapid "betterment" of the future lives of we two brothers. For a reason which you will soon discover, gentle reader, I now believe that such speculation has a sound basis – a basis which will, I trust, become clearer from the remaining passages of this chapter.

So much, indeed, did I regard Mr P as being the epitome of kindness that when I decided to "run away" from home one evening and to take my brother along with me, it was to Mr P's big house that we hotfooted it in order to seek alternative shelter! I must have done something very naughty at home (the details of which, if I did do so, I have long since forgotten) which had upset, or "vexed", Joanna or Maas Bab and had probably received the "tammun whip" one too many times for my liking. At any rate, we ran away from Joanna's custody for the first and only time that I can remember and went off to Mr P's place. He readily took us in - without much persuasion or otherwise on my part, as I recollect. But he must have developed "cold feet" overnight - by, perhaps, becoming pre-occupied with thoughts of the major consequences for him and his career as Montserrat's Magistrate if it ever came out that he was allowing two small boys to live with him in his big house. So, I seem to remember, he gently and successfully persuaded us, in the morning, of the wisdom of returning home to face Joanna and "the music" - or, rather and almost certainly, the tammun whip and even more "lashes"! But he must, firstly, have sworn John and myself to secrecy, regarding our not revealing to anyone where we had in fact spent the night. When we got home, Joanna, of course, very much wanted to know (or, more likely, _demanded_ to be told) exactly where we had been all night long. I continually told the lie (and John must have backed me up on this) that we had slept in one of our farmstead's fields, sheltered by the thick stalks of sugar cane growing within it. So, once again, my pilfered book of fairy tales might have come in useful - not least, this time, for prompting me to take elements from the story of Hansel and Gretel losing their way in the forest and how they had managed to survive overnight.

As I write of these days of my early life in Montserrat, I am starting to realise that, from about the age of five to eight years or so, I had committed so many "mortal sins" - for example, in relation to my lies to Joanna and that purloined book of fairy tales - that I must be appearing to my reader as being the very antithesis of what a good little Catholic schoolboy should have been like. Thus, that teacher of mine, from my junior school days in Plymouth all those years ago, must have been very perceptive in casting me as Lucifer in the Adam and Eve school play - of which I have dealt earlier in this chapter and in which, it will be remembered, that I performed so devilishly bad.

More than likely, my running away with my little brother, for one whole night, had been the final straw for my great-grandmother and Maas Bab. I can still recall her saying: *"Me no ear-bell!"*. That is to say, that she was no longer "able", or felt fit enough, to look after us. I do not remember if this was actually said by her on the morning that John and I returned from our running away, but it certainly would have been a most appropriate occasion on which to say it. For she would have been at least about 65 years of age by then. Any frustration or alarm at my (and John's) unruliness at this time would have been strengthened in Joanna by her possibly hearing rumours of little David and John spending time inside "the Batty Man's" house. For such was the expression which I seem to recollect the older boys in my Amersham neighbourhood calling someone of Mr P's proclivities - sometimes, perhaps, after they saw us emerging from a visit to his house. For, in our local Montserratian dialect, "batty" meant a person's bottom or posterior. Our community's expression, therefore, did not extend to any word so complicated as the term "paedophile" - an expression which is very commonly used in the "standard English" of my Cambridge life in 2008 as I write this volume. At any rate, before I was nine years old, Joanna (with or without Maas Bab's backing) was taking concrete steps to send John and I to our parents in England! Perhaps, they had simply complained to our parents (by letter) of how unruly John and I had become - or, on the other hand, the initiative to "send for" us two boys might have come spontaneously, and coincidentally at this time of our running away, from those parents to our great-grandmother and her husband back in Montserrat. Whatever the source of the initiative, however, the fact was that we had more than likely outgrown our little triangular area of familiarity - perhaps, both geographically and mentally - and it was time for us to expand our horizons by "flying the nest" and the confines of our very island itself.

(m) *"Doctors and nurses" (and beyond?)*

It would be wrong for me to give the impression that Mr P was the only person in Montserrat who had had a hand in introducing me to human sexual matters during my boyhood years on my native island. This is owing to the fact that, on the contrary, I had already been exposed (to some small extent) to some of the "goings on" involved in heterosexual activity by some of the bigger boys in my immediate neighbourhood. For those lads would get some of our little girl neighbours, of about the same age as me I suppose, to show me (and perhaps John, who was usually with me at the time) their private parts - both external (which we called the "porky", pronounced "pworky", or "poom-poom") and the more internal aspects - in return for my showing my privates (which in Montserratian dialect I would refer to as my "tally") to the relevant little girl or girls at the time. In this context, I can still particularly recall the amusing expression "skinning out" from those days. Even worse than engaging in such relatively innocent exercises of "doctors and nurses", however, was the fact that some of these older boys (whom I see now must have been considerably experienced in sexual activity with girls closer in age to their own but which "young ladies" were nevertheless probably no older than early teenagers), would try to egg me on (and perhaps John also) to try to have intercourse itself with these younger girls of no more than six or seven. It is most unlikely, therefore, that we ever succeeded in fully complying with such peer group coercion.

David R. Bradshaw

Chapter 3:
Taking Leave of My Sensible Horizons

(a) Getting immunised and luggage-buying

I do not know whether Joanna ever became aware of my "quasi-medical" activities with some of the local children of Amersham. Nor, indeed, of the extent to which the sightings of my brother and I frequenting Mr P's house ever reached her from the report of any of our neighbours. But, as stated, my running away from home for one night - with my little brother in tow - must have been something amounting to "the straw which broke the camel's back" for my great-grandmother and Maas Bab. Thus, during a time when I was still in the junior section of my school, I can remember that John and I had to go to visit a doctor's office in order to receive our vaccinations. This process was a pre-requisite to our being allowed to travel from Montserrat abroad. Indeed, as if all my fairy-tale "three wishes" had all come true at once, my brother and I were suddenly informed by Joanna, one day, that we would soon be leaving home, and Montserrat itself, to go to England – permanently! I can still now recall walking with John across the large playing field at the back of my junior school section and in a direction away from my classroom (and our church) and towards the centre of Plymouth, in order to take a short cut to our doctor's office. Some time off from lessons, surely, but what ordeals lay ahead in those medical offices to which we were then headed?

I recall being very worried at the time about the pain which I would have to suffer in order to obtain the required vaccination. This is because I already knew that I hated having injections - perhaps from my experience of visiting the hospital when I had nearly "chopped off" my left foot. And a vaccination was, I had been led to believe, much worse than an injection. At all events, whatever pain we were in fact subjected to, both John and I duly received our immunity-giving jabs. It may have been administered by a female nurse, a member of a class which I much prefer, even today, to male doctors. And I am even able to recall having to have the site of the jab's placement covered over with a bit of pink "sticking plaster". We then had to wait a number of days – or, perhaps, even up to a fortnight - in order to see whether the vaccination had "taken". I also seem to remember that for one of us, and I cannot now recall whether it was in relation to John or myself, this "taking" did not happen the first time and that one brother had to have the "operation" repeated. At any rate, eventually both of us, on further visits to the doctor's office, were pronounced to have been properly immunised and had, thus, overcome one more hurdle to our being able to leave Montserrat and join our parents in England. But, along with the scar on my left instep, I would now be leaving with another permanent reminder of my schooldays in Montserrat. This was, and still is, the small indentations on the outside-middle of my upper-left arm, caused by that major assault upon my little person - namely, the infliction of that smallpox, or polio, vaccination.

I also remember that associated with the immunisation processes, in preparation for our departure from Montserrat, was the need for us to buy a suitcase (or, perhaps, one each for John and myself - though with only one pair of shoes each (which fitted), I would have thought that one such item, only, would have been quite sufficient). We called such piece of luggage a "grip" - possibly because of the way the lid-part of the suitcase secured itself to the larger voluminous counterpart by way of the two sets of latching devices situated on each of the two separate parts. I cannot now actually remember going into any of the few shops in Plymouth which would have stocked such luggage, but I can imagine that it must have been very exciting for us boys to be going shopping with Joanna for our grip or grips for the very first, and majorly significant, overseas trip of our lives. Such a prospect should have been even more exhilarating than going to Bata's in town to shop for the annual pair of shoes for church and the taking of that photograph for our parents in England, where, by the grace of some fairy-godmother or other, we ourselves were soon to be headed.

(b) Presents _from_ the teacher

I have written earlier that I do not any longer recall any of my teachers from my schooldays in Montserrat - whether in the infants' section, or the juniors proper across the road next to St Patrick's Church. Whilst this is strictly true in relation to my actually sitting in a classroom and being taught the rudiments of the three R's - and whilst, perversely, I do recall using my own personal slate and chalk, as well as the abacus, in those learning processes - my earlier statement requires a little qualification. This is because there was, in fact, one teacher who was evidently fond of both John and myself and who wanted to give each of us something to remember her by. I am pretty sure that she was not even my own teacher at the time of our leaving the school and our island. However, she may well have been John's, for I seem to recall that she was based in a classroom situated in his infants' section of the school. Her name was Sister Marie-Sylvie. I was to find out, many years later, that she was one of several teacher-nuns from Belgium - indeed from the famous beer-making city (or town) of Leuven or Louvain - who were based at the convent adjacent to the our schools infants' section, and of which convent the private school (previously referred to in Chapter 2 above) formed a part.

I remember the Sister's name extremely well, even today, because of the leaving presents which she gave to John and myself. In my case, she gave a piece of gold jewellery. I think it may well have been a cross. But, alas, I have long since lost or misplaced this gift during the ensuing 50 years or so since my receiving it. My brother's present, however, is the key to my vague memory of our teacher-nun - for it was a small picture of the Sacred Heart of Jesus, on the back of which the kind religious lady had written words along the lines of: *"To little John Bradshaw ...from Sister Marie-Sylvie"*. She may have also written a few additional words and included a date - but the essentials of her hand-written words on John's gift are those which I have just quoted. I would be surprised if my brother still has that little picture today, but for many years it adorned the mantelpiece of our parents' home in England - that is to say, the house in which we were to continue our later growing up into adolescence, and beyond, once we had emigrated from Montserrat.

(c) The ticket to travel and the acquiring of a minder for the passage

One of the major preparations which had to be made for our departure from our native island stemmed from the fact that we would be travelling as two small children without either parent. Indeed, we would be making our momentous voyage without the company of any relative at all - for our local "nearest and dearest", Joanna and Maas Bab, were not going to escort us on our expedition across the Atlantic Ocean to England. Rather, they were staying put in Montserrat - the island of their own births also, and which they had probably never left the shores of in their, then already, long lives. So, either out of family prudence for our safety during the voyage, or because of the shipping company's policy against children travelling unaccompanied, or, possibly, for some other reason, some adult had to be found who could "mind" us during our trip. I do not know whether Joanna and Maas Bab had a difficult job finding a suitable (grown-up) candidate, whom they knew, who would also be travelling to England on the same ship as John and myself. But, at any rate, a gentleman by the name of "Harold" accepted to take on the role of being our "chaperone" for the journey and safe delivery to our parents. And, thus, eventually everything was in place for us to take our very first trip outside our native island – indeed, one of our very first "outings" from our little "triangle area of familiarity" district which I have tried to describe earlier.

Most fortunately, even after these 50 or so years have passed since the Montserrat departure of John and myself, I still have in my possession the ticket issued by the shipping firm in question for our transatlantic passage (see Fig 17 below).

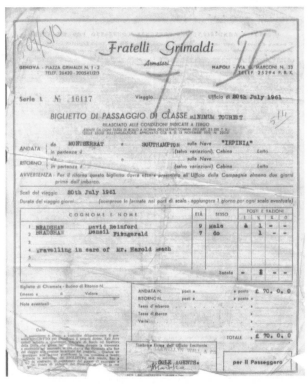

Fig 17: The "passage" ticket from Montserrat, West Indies to Southampton, England, on the *Irpinia*, for David and John dated 20 July, 1961

That nautical concern was the "Fratelli Grimaldi" - which I now know means the Grimaldi Brothers - of both Genoa and Naples, in Italy. The ticket is dated 20 July 1961. It did not, however, originate directly from the aforementioned Italian firm. Rather, it is stamped by the *"Firma dell'Ufficio Emittente"* - which I understand to mean the (local) booking agents – namely, "W. LLEWELLYN WALL & CO". These local agents would have been based in Plymouth, Montserrat, I would suppose. But whoever signed-off the ticket on behalf of such local firm went to the trouble of also making sure that it was also typed on the ticket, in English, that the firm was acting as "SOLE AGENTS". The ticket is a pro-forma printed in the Italian language, with the gaps of the pro-forma filled in - in English. These completed details include certain facts, such as the names of the passengers being "David Reinford Bradshaw" and "Densil Fitzgerald Bradshaw" who were of the "Male" *"sesso"* and whose *"età"* were "9" (sic) and "7" years old, respectively.

In relation to my brother's name, I was surprised to see (on looking at the ticket again after all these years) that he is not named as I have always thought he was officially registered at birth - namely, as *"John* Denzil Bradshaw". On querying this apparent mistake with my brother recently (in March 2008), much to my complete surprise, he was able to explain the discrepancy. For he told me that the ticket did, in fact, state his name correctly! This is because that stated name was, indeed, the one originally given to him at birth - and, thus, must have been communicated by Joanna to the local shipping agents as being John's "official" name – for the purpose of international travel and the like. Joanna, according to John, had however been calling him by a different name at home for many years prior to the time of our emigration. For my brother had, in some way or other, reminded Joanna of her own dead son, and former steel band player, John - the one who had died through his nail biting, according to my great-grandmother - and she had simply wanted to preserve his memory by re-naming a young, living, person after her own dearly departed offspring. In time, my brother acquired the name "John" by force of usage alone - and not by the sudden legal process of a change by deed poll - and a, slightly different, form of his original *first* name, "Densil", also (over time) became his *middle* name.

Our "*BILGLIETTO DI PASSAGGIO*", or ticket of passage, also states that both John and I were travelling at half fares or "*posti*", that we were booked for the "*andata*" or outward voyage but not the "*ritorno*", and that the total cost of this one-way ticket was the then-princely sum of seventy pounds, no shillings and no pence (£70.0.0). It also states that, for that price, we were to travel in the "MINIMUM TOURIST" *classe*. Most importantly, the ticket stated that the one-way journey which John and I were booked on was '*da MONTSERRAT a SOUTHAMPTON sulla Nave "IRPINIA"*'. An additional piece of very significant information, which I had not suspected was still extant anywhere in the world, is stated on the face of the ticket, in English. This is that we two boy passengers would be "Travelling in care of Mr. Harold *Roach*"!

Grimaldi-Siosa Lines	
Sailings September 1963-August 1964 (issued September 1963)	
Vessel(s)	**Ports of call**
Irpinia	Typical voyage: Westbound: Genoa, Cannes, Barcelona, Tenerife, Martinique, Trinidad, La Guaira. Eastbound: La Guaira, Guadeloupe, Tenerife, Barcelona, Cannes, Genoa. Additional ports of call on other voyages: Las Palmas, Guadeloupe and Barbados westbound; Trinidad, Grenada, Martinique, Dominica and Antigua eastbound. One roundtrip sailing in December/January: La Guaira, Curaçao, Kingston, Tenerife, Madeira, Lisbon, Vigo, Le Havre, Southampton and v.v.

Fig 18: Poster for a contemporary *Irpinia* voyage - but one which was scheduled for just over two years later than that taken by David and John. It is only *an example* of such *Irpinia* publicity for the early 1960s (not an advertisement for the specific (August 1961) Montserrat to Southampton voyage in question). (The sailing schedule, and related brochure, are used with the kind permission of Mr Björn Larrsen and are from his collection. The "Introduction" page of his "Maritime Timetable Images" website can be found at: http://www.timetableimages.com/maritime/index.htm)

One vital piece of data, however, appears to be missing from the ticket. This is the <u>start date</u> of our one-way journey from Montserrat to Southampton on the "*Irpinia*". And insofar as the wording on the ticket, "*Scali del viaggio*", is meant to refer to such starting date, that date cannot in fact have been the date on which we left our island, for it is stated to be "20th July 1961" - the very same date as that stated to be the *date of issue of the ticket*. I am sure, however, that my very serious, and no-nonsense, great-grandmother, Joanna, would have purchased the ticket, and would have kept it safely in her possession for us boys, *some weeks before* the ship arrived in Plymouth for us to start our epic journey to England.

At any rate, whatever the mystery of our voyage's "start date" as stated on the ticket, the great day eventually came for our departure. But, in fact, it was not a "day" at all - but, rather, a Montserratian late evening, or "night" as the locals would have called it. For we must only have had *approximate* timings of when the ship, on which we were travelling, would arrive at the port in Plymouth to pick up those passengers travelling from Montserrat to England - including, of course, us two small Bradshaw boys and our adult minder, Harold. I seem to recall being dressed by Joanna, in preparation for the trip, on the morning of the day on which the ship had been announced as being due to arrive at Plymouth's port - and then spending all day long looking for a big vessel steaming towards that port from some point in the Kinsale direction. I also recollect continuing such "look out" process into the evening, and then, long past sunset. All four members of the Brumble household constantly stared into the gloom out at sea, in a south-easterly direction, for any sign at all of that much awaited vessel. At long, long last, we saw the lights of a great "hotel-on-the-high-seas" ship - our ocean liner, the *Nave "Irpinia"*.

(d) The leaving of Joanna and Maas Bab

Joanna and Maas Bab must have had a taxi waiting on standby to take us, and our luggage, at very short notice to the port in Plymouth - once the ship was spotted. For a hired vehicle did come quickly, I seem to recall. One might have thought that both Joanna and Maas Bab would then have accompanied us in that taxi for one last time. Alas, neither of them did so! I have tried to remind myself of the reason for this - without success. Certainly, I do not think that it was because of the number of "grips", which we two boys had had to carry with us, taking up all the capacity in the taxi (which should otherwise have been able to accommodate at least two more adult passengers). For, as stated earlier, we poor lads needed no more than one largish suitcase, to share, for our few possessions - or, certainly, no more than one small one each. Rather, I think it more likely that Joanna may have been through too many such previous occasions of saying long "goodbyes" to her nearest and dearest who were emigrating to England. This is because it is likely that she would have suffered such a process with her own daughters Mary (my grandmother), "Auntie" Queen, "Auntie" Esther, her own son "Uncle" Ben, and with her granddaughter Margaret (my own mother). To, therefore, voluntarily go through the same, potentially traumatic, parting process once more at the port with the two little boys she had so recently raised from babyhood may have been just one, self-imposed, emotional trauma too far. We, thus, took our leave of Joanna and Maas Bab outside their chattel house in Amersham - that little movable construction which had also been the secure foundation, indeed "home" and "nest", for us two boys for the past seven years or so (which was as long a period as we could ever remember and which therefore, effectively, amounted to each of our conscious "lifetimes").

More than likely Joanna (and possibly also Maas Bab) cried during that parting process. I cannot recall exactly what happened during the saying of our "goodbyes" and possibly - for the first time ever, perhaps - the embracing and kissing of each other fervently, before John and I got into our waiting taxi. But I am pretty sure that I, for one, did not cry. For I would most likely have been extremely excited about taking the biggest step so far in my then relatively short life - namely, going on a big ship, across miles and miles of ocean, and finally meeting up, in England, with my mother and father whom I had not seen for years and years and whom I could not even remember in any sense at all. Just as exciting, would have been the prospect of meeting my "baby" brother, George, who had been born in London on 6 February 1956 and who was, at the time of our leaving Montserrat, aged only five years old. I had only seen one photograph of George before our departure, as far as I can remember. This showed him sitting in someone's garden on his little tricycle - a "toy". The prospect of, perhaps soon, getting one of those playthings for John and myself (even to share), would have been the most lovely dream for me at the time! The seriousness of the occasion of my parting from Joanna did not pass me by, however. For, before boarding our taxi, I made Joanna a solemn promise. What that promise was, I will say more about - but only later on in this chapter.

(e) Getting aboard, for abroad

When we arrived at Plymouth port, I can recall a scene of pandemonium. It was still night time and, therefore, the place was in relative darkness and there were people milling about everywhere. Some of these would have been fellow passengers. But there would also have been as many, or even more, persons seeing their loved ones off. There present, also, would have been other taxi drivers who had transported some of the throng - as well as workers at the port such as the loaders of the passengers' luggage, general stevedores employed for loading and unloading non-passenger cargo, and boatmen generally. Out of the *pot-pourri* of all these people, I am pretty sure that John and I had to find, or link up with, just one of them - namely, our minder Harold - and *vice versa*. This is owing to the fact that I do not recall that he travelled with us during the taxi ride down the hill from Amersham. Perhaps, Joanna had charged our taxi driver with doing the necessary bringing together of the parties - for surely, in the confusion of persons around us, John and I would not have been able (or properly equipped) to achieve such a feat by ourselves alone. At any rate, the two sets of, would-be, transatlantic passengers must have eventually found each other and, presently, John and I could take our final steps on Montserrat's soil for, what might well have been, our very last time.

As it turned out, these final steps were not to be those of simply proceeding along the Plymouth jetty, up a gangway of the waiting, and anchored, *Irpinia* and then a transfer to its deck at the top of those steps. Rather, John and I (with Harold and our respective sets of luggage) had to go to a point, somewhere near the end of the jetty, in order to be lowered - and, I seem to remember, more being manhandled downwards at some speed by a number of burly men - into a waiting small rowing boat. For the Plymouth port was not a deep water harbour - as obtains, to my knowledge, in some of the other islands such as that at Bridgetown in Barbados. This means that large ocean-going liners such as the *Irpinia* could not, at that time, come in very close to the shoreline and any available jetty - for to do so would be to risk running aground. Accordingly, small boats - called "lighters", in standard English, I understand - had to take the passengers and their luggage from the shore (or available jetty) out to the ship lying at anchor, perhaps some 100 yards or more from the point of departure. And that "lighter-transfer-process" is exactly what John, Harold and I had to go through that particular dark night when the *Irpinia* came - along with several other passengers in the same, or in one of several other similar, little rowing boat (as well as all our respective luggage). I can certainly remember such transfer process, in our specific case, being quite chaotic. For we first had to get into our designated little boat, which was not an easy task, given that it was rocking from the waves under it - despite being temporarily tethered to the Plymouth jetty. Moreover, it was difficult to see exactly what we were doing, since it was not a moonlit night. Further still, we had to carry into the boat, and find space for, our "grips" and other luggage - as well as ourselves. And, then again, there was the fact that we had to reverse such processes once we had been rowed out to the ship - including disembarking from our little lighter, which was by then, perhaps, rocking even harder, owing to the deeper water in which the ship lay at anchor - and then, somehow, climb up its shaky (temporarily deployed) steps from our little ferry boat to the ship's main deck, along with our grips and other impedimenta. Given the *mêlée* that all our boarding stages entailed that night, it is perhaps not difficult to see why these happenings left an indelible impression in my still developing memory and thirst for new experiences.

Once on board the *Irpinia* - and it must have been close to midnight, or later, by the time that we finally made it up from our individual lighter to the top of the steps which had been positioned over the side of the ship - we had to find the accommodation which had been allocated to John and myself. The pro-forma ticket for our passage, which I referred to earlier, in fact leaves blank the gaps (which were to be completed) for the number of our "*Cabina*" and that of our respective bed or "*Letto*". However, there *is* to be found, noted in red crayon on the face of the ticket, certain numbers, as follows: "7 II". Moreover, in much smaller handwriting and written in pencil, are the numbers "5/4". There is a third set of numbers, written in ballpoint this time, and of a size between the crayon and pencil numbers: this final set refers to "509/510" - which could perhaps have been the passenger numbers of John and myself. These various numberings may thus indicate exactly where we had been put inside the ship. At any rate, our actual placing on the ship turned out to be some kind of group cabin, or dormitory, into which perhaps 10 or more bunk beds were squeezed into a relatively small space. Worse still, the cabin was somewhere near the bottom of the ship - which meant that the atmosphere there was usually rather warm in temperature. Worst of all, our "minimum tourist" accommodation meant that we had been given an "inside" cabin and, thus, that we had no windows nor portholes from which to get a view to the outside world, or even a little bit of ventilation when the immediate environment within got too hot or stuffy.

Once we had, eventually, found our cabin, Harold instructed us as to which of the several beds therein were to be ours. I seem to recall that John and I were not allowed by him to have any of the upper bunks - much as I, in my usual adventurous vein, would have wanted to have had one (at least for myself) - whatever the risk may have been of my falling out of it whilst asleep. I also seem to recall that all the fellow passengers with us in our cabin were all adults and all of the male sex. One might well anticipate that with a number of healthy young men occupying the cabin, full of excitement and the sense of adventure regarding their new (albeit temporary) life on the ocean waves, our single-sex accommodation was not very likely to remain that way, for very long, throughout the voyage to England!

Sleep must have quickly come upon me that night - after all the excitements of the previous day, evening and the earlier part of it. For, I can still recall that the next morning seemed to arrive quickly and that I was soon up on deck, with some other adult passengers standing nearby, and with all of us looking at the island of Montserrat some few miles away. Evidently, after loading up with its passengers from our island during the night, the *Irpinia* had not immediately sailed on to its next port of call. Rather, it was only just starting to do so about the time that I happened to venture up to the main deck for the first time in daylight. Whilst surveying the scene with such other passengers - of the longish, bumpy and greyish-black shape of my native island - I heard one of them utter some words to the effect that Montserrat had got its name: "because it looks like a rat. A monster rat!". I had not heard that unforgettable explanation ever given to me before - whether from any of my teachers at St Augustine's RC School or otherwise. So I did not even begin to take the adult's explanation too seriously - even then, when I was still less than nine years old. Rather, I would, very probably, upon looking at my island for one last time, have been seriously wondering along the following lines: "Will I ever be back to see my native land again? Will I ever be able to carry out my solemn promise to my great-grandmother on leaving her by taxi the night before – namely, to come back one day and see her again? …to keep my word to 'my great-grandmother who had mothered me' – Miss Joanna?"

PLYMOUTH, MONTSERRAT.

Fig 19: Sketch of the view looking towards the harbour of Plymouth, Montserrat – showing jetty and hinterland (including, possibly, St Patrick's RC Church with spire in the left of the sketch just above the jetty) in or before 1889. The view is not that different from that which the author remembers, about 70 years later, from the *Irpinia* in 1961 as he looked back to shore on the morning after boarding the ship for England the previous night. The sketch is from Owen T Bulkeley's 1889 book entitled *"The Lesser Antilles. A guide for settlers in the British West Indies and tourist companion"*.

David R. Bradshaw

Montserrat, W.I.

Fig 19A: A copy of a postcard showing "Port Plymouth before and after volcanic activities". © Kevin West, of Paradise Photo and Art Studio, Montserrat, West Indies – and used with his kind permission. In the top, "Before the volcano", photo - to the upper right of the image - can be seen the Soufriere Hills. In front of those Hills (as the viewer looks upwards towards them) is where the hamlet of Amersham is situated – and where the author and his little brother, John, grew up BAREFOOT during the late 1950s and early 60s. In the bottom photo, a white plume of "ash", spewing out of the Soufriere Hills volcano, can be clearly seen.

Irpinia (Grimaldi-SIOSA: 1955-1981)

The *Irpinia* was built as the SGTM liner *Campana* in 1929 by Swan, Hunter [sic] on the River Tyne. She sailed from Marseille to the East Coast of South America, Rio de Janeiro, Santos, Montevideo and Buenos Aires. After the fall of France in 1940, *Campana* was laid up at the latter port, and later seized by the Argentineans, for whom she ran some trips to New Orleans as the *Rio Jachal*. In 1946, she was returned to the French, sailing to South America again, but also to Indochina. She was bought by Grimaldi-SIOSA in 1955. She operated from Europe to the Caribbean and Venezuela, with some crossings of the North Atlantic to Canada or New York. In 1962 she received a major facelift, returning to service with only one funnel and Fiat diesels instead of steam turbines. She returned to the Caribbean route, taking Spanish and Portuguese migrants westbound, and west Indian [sic] migrants eastbound to the UK. By 1970 she was mainly used for Mediterranean cruising out of Genoa, at $79 for seven days, or $134 for a 2-week Christmas cruise to New York and the Canaries. In 1976, just as she was about to be withdrawn, she was chartered for the making of the film *Voyage of the Damned*. After the filming, she unexpectedly returned to cruising until 1981, at which point she could no longer get a certificate of seaworthiness in Italy. She was laid up for 2 years in La Spezia before being scrapped.

The picture below shows *Irpinia's* original two-funnelled state, on a card giving the company's full title: Fratelli Grimaldi - Sicula Oceanica S.A.

A second Grimaldi postcard of *Irpinia in* original two-funnelled state.

Fig 20: Extract from a website detailing the history of the *Irpinia* and showing two different postcards of the fine, two-

funnelled, state in which she had been (when David and John voyaged on her from Montserrat to England in August 1961). The extract, including the postcards, is used with the kind permission of Mr Ian Boyle of Simplon Postcards. His website can be found at: www.simplonpc.co.uk

Chapter 4:
Back before the Future

(a) My father's extended (and "extensive") family

I t seems right that, before I (hopefully, one day, very soon) chronicle what further happened on board the *Irpinia* on my way to Southampton, England - and then of my subsequent history in my adopted country - I go back to the issue of where I came from. That is to say, how I came to be born in Montserrat in the first place. This is because, thus far, I have concentrated mainly on but one side of my family roots - namely that of Margaret, my mother. But, of course, there is also my derivation from the side of my father, James, to be taken into account - if I am to give a balanced picture of my *fons et origo*.

As I write, I have "an exact and true copy" of my father's birth entry in the official records of Montserrat. That copy, or "birth certificate", evidences "Entry No 48/1242 of 1926 in the Register of Births, District "A", Montserrat. It states that his name is "James Alfred", that he was born on the 20th of May 1926 at "Dyer's" and that his mother's name is "Mary Ryan". It also attests that he was born "Illegitimate" and, just to underline this fact, to the pro-forma question as to whether James' parents were married at the time of his birth, the answer "No" has been completed in black ink. Worse still, to the pro-forma's section asking for the details of James' own father to be provided, there is to be seen a line inserted - also in black - as if to say that the issue of James' paternity was irrelevant, or at least not important, in his case.

But, of course, the issue of his paternity was of vital importance to my father. For it is noticeable that nowhere on his birth certificate does the name "Bradshaw" appear. Yet, that was the surname which he was to adhere to during his life - that is to say, the surname of his own natural father, one "Joseph Bradshaw". As I understand matters, in Montserrat, at the time of my father's birth (and during his early years of growing up there) if a child was born illegitimate it was common for only its mother's name to be entered on its birth certificate and for the child to bear its mother's surname thereafter. That is, therefore, what might well have happened in my father's case - given the state of his birth certificate as I have just described it. But, clearly, someone from the time of his early life must have had other ideas - and my father stuck with one of these other ways of doing things when he became old enough to decide for himself what he wished his surname to be for his future life.

We have thus seen that my own father's parents were not married at the time of his birth. Nor were they ever to be so during their lives. That is not to say that Joseph and Mary failed to emulate their New Testament namesakes in their closeness to each other. For, on the contrary, so closely connected were they in fact that they were to produce at least *eight* other living children, in addition to my father James, during the period of their cohabitation in Dyer's Village, Montserrat. Indeed, my father was not even one of the first of these total of nine offspring. For it appears that he was only the fourth of his parents' seven sons - and even his only surviving sister was also born before him. Thus, in the order of their respective births as far as I have been able to glean the facts, the nine were as follows: George, Joe, Mary, William ("Willy"), Martha (who, alas, died whilst a teenager), my father (James, "Jim" or "Jimmy"), John (who also died young, whilst still living at home), Tom and "Hammy" (Abraham). As already stated, my father was born in 1926. His younger brother Tom was born almost exactly three years later on the 12th of May 1929. Hammy, the baby of the family, was born almost two years after Tom on the 11th of April 1931. Hammy was thus almost five years younger than my father, Jim. Going the other way, my father's only surviving sister, Mary, was born on the 26th of July 1919, and his immediately elder surviving brother, Willy, was born on the 30th of August 1921. These two last-mentioned siblings are thus, respectively, about seven and five years older than my father. Of the nine, only Tom and George (so far as I know, and without taking their two early-deceased siblings, Martha and John, into account) took their mother's surname (of "Ryan") as their own during their lives. But, it appears (and I will be coming back to this anon), that, at least one of my Uncle Tom's own sons used the surname of the father of Tom and his siblings for at least a part of that son's adult life.

Thus my grandfather, Joseph, spawned a large family - by today's standards at any rate. But to stop with his nine offspring just mentioned would be to tell but half the story. This is because he also had *another family* with a different woman from my grandmother, Mary! This other woman was named Catherine. Moreover, unlike the case with Mary, Joseph had given a greater token of his affections for Catherine by also going to the trouble of making an "honest woman" of her. This, of course, was by marrying Catherine along the way - whether before or after the first member of the "legitimate" brood of Bradshaws had been born into the world. For, according to my uncle Hammy and his wife, my aunt Amelia (who incidentally is also my great-aunt by blood, she being the half-sister of my *maternal* grandmother, Mary) - whom I met with and interviewed on Saturday the 8th of March 2008, at their home in Stoke Newington, London - Joseph and Catherine had had about 10 or more children in their ("legitimate") brood! These included my aunt Martha, who was also to emigrate to England and eventually settle there in the Leicester area. There was also my uncle Ernest, whom I never knew but who fathered (among others) two female cousins who also ended up settling in England (that is to say, London, in their particular case) – namely, Cousin Rebecca Bradshaw and Cousin Elaine Daley (*née* Bradshaw, and also known as "Mem", after her father Ernest's full-sister of the same name). Those first cousins of mine, in turn, were to have their own offspring – who are also my first cousins, but "once removed" in their case - some of whom I was to get to know particularly well during my early, or later, life in England, not least: Rebecca's eldest daughter, the late Catherine Bradshaw who died much too prematurely in her early twenties; and Elaine's daughter, Lazelle Daley, who at one time worked for many years in the BBC's Drama department in White City, London.

According to Uncle Hammy and Aunt Amelia (who is also known by her formal name of "Catherine" or "Cathy") - and much to my surprise - my grandfather Joseph did not originate from Montserrat at all! Rather, he and three (according to Hammy), or two (according to his older brother, my uncle Willy), of his brothers had migrated from their native island of Barbados in order to settle in Montserrat. Indeed, according to these close relatives of mine, until those brothers came to Montserrat there were no Bradshaws on the island at all. Thus, this means that the *fons et origo* of the Bradshaw name in Montserrat lies with those brothers - and not, for example, because of the close connection which Montserrat also has with the European country of Ireland[7] and from which latter country may well originate similar sounding surnames which are well-known on my native island, such as "Brades" and "Brady".

Corroboration of the Barbados origins of the Montserrat Bradshaws was provided, just prior to the publication of this book, by one of Uncle Tom's Swindon-based sons, on the eve of 10.10.10 - or the 10th of October 2010 – which just happened to be the corroborator's 61st birthday, *as well as the date of Auntie Martin's sad passing*. This person is Cousin "Parpa" (aka Emmanuel Joseph Cabey) who told me that when our common paternal grandmother, Miss Baby, was growing frail in later life, and could no longer go to the Plymouth market to sell produce from the Bradshaws' lands in Dyers, he would organise such selling, for her, through the wife of his father's eldest brother, Uncle George, whose name was Aunt "Henny", or Henrietta. Through such collaboration, he

---

[7] For a good background on Montserrat's strong Irish heritage, see (among others): John C. Messenger "Montserrat: 'The Most Distinctively Irish Settlement in the New World'", ETHNICITY 2, 281-303 (1975)

(Par-pa) became close to his grandmother and it was she who revealed to him that her partner, and our common grandfather, Joseph Leacock Bradshaw, and his siblings (including the "dark" Jimmy who settled in Salem, Montserrat), originally came from Barbados.

Going back to what Uncle Hammy and Aunt Amelia told me in 2008, two of the immigrating brothers from Barbados, Joseph and George, put down their roots in the Dyer's area. And whilst my grandfather took up the occupation of cultivating land in that area (of his own, or that leased from the Griffin family according to Uncle Hammy, among others), his brother George (and his wife) operated a general shop or store from his home in the Dyer's area alongside his other "trade" of being a cobbler. However, according to Hammy's elder brother, Willy, whom I interviewed at his home in Stamford Hill, London on Saturday the 15th of March 2008, Grandfather Joseph did not merely content himself with "cultivating the ground" in Dyer's. He also actively practised his trade of being a "great" (according to Uncle Willy, who had, perhaps, meant "master") carpenter who, during his professional career, had contributed to the building of Government House in Montserrat - a trade which he might well have learned, or fine-tuned, earlier in his life when he had (also according to Uncle Willy) worked on the building of the Panama Canal on the mainland of Central America.

Fig 20A: A copy of a postcard showing Montserrat's beautiful and ornate Government House. (Photo by Tommie Reardon. Pub by Mc-Hen, Montserrat, W.I.). Did the author's paternal grandfather, Joseph Leacock Bradshaw, really contribute, through his master carpenter's skills, to the creation of this work of art? The author would really like to believe so!

Fig 20B: A photo showing Montserrat's former beautiful and ornate Government House – post the Volcano – and as reduced to a shadow of its former glory. The photo was sent to the author by fellow-Montserratian, and fellow Old-St Augustian (of Plymouth, Montserrat), Lecretia ("Mary") Lindsay on 6 January 2010 – as part of her New Year greeting to the author and her other email contacts.

Such must have been the different accent and other ways of Joseph (and his brother George) compared to the local indigenous Dyer's people that Uncle Hammy well recalls one of Joseph's good friends (one Jack Gibbons) calling Joseph by the nickname "Bajy" (pronounced "beer-gee")! (Uncle Hammy told me that he, too, got landed with this nickname by some of the people in Dyer's at the time, apparently because he resembled his father, my grandfather, so closely). The other two (according to Uncle Hammy), or one (according to Uncle Willy), Barbadian (or "Bajan") Bradshaw brothers, however, settled in the Salem area of Montserrat and neither my Aunt Amelia nor Uncle Hammy, alas, can recall much information about them - including what their Christian names, or occupations, were. Fortunately, I have been able to successfully track down a direct descendant, living in London, of one of the original Bajan Bradshaws who settled in Salem (always remembering that, as stated, Uncle Hammy claims that there were, in fact, *two* of these) - in the person of Pastor Danny Bradshaw. Danny was able to confirm (during my interview with him at his home in Enfield, north London, on Saturday the 10th of May 2008) that this third brother, of Salem, was named James (or "Jimmy", as my own father was also, later in the 20th century, to be affectionately called) and that he, Danny, is the grandson of Jimmy of Salem – who had illegitimately fathered one Arthur Bradshaw (among others), Danny's own father.

My own grandfather, Joseph, must have been quite a remarkable man. For not only did he "keep" two families on the go at the same time, but also he managed to have those families living side-by-side with each other within the Dyer's community - in evident harmony! Both Uncle Hammy and Uncle Willy have related to me that the two separate households were no more than a matter of yards apart. Indeed, Willy was even able to tell me that the two *ménages* were so close to each other that one of the matriarchs could stand on her doorstep, shout to the other mother, and be easily heard by that other on her own doorstep! Moreover, the two heads of household – my *paternal* grandmother, Mary (whom Uncle Hammy and Aunt Amelia distinctly recall being generally referred to, by all around her, by the nicknames of "Baby Saywell", "Miss Baby" or just "Babes"), and Joseph's wife, Catherine - overlapped in their production of children for Joseph during their respective periods of child-rearing. And though Catherine, it seems, was to give birth to a greater number of live and surviving children for Joseph, my grandmother Mary - according to Uncle Hammy's daughter, and my first cousin, Gloria, from Gloria's conversations with our mutual aunt, Mary ("Mrs Martin" or "Auntie Martin"), prior to the latter suffering a most debilitating stroke in February 2008 which, effectively, robbed her of the ability to speak - had also had about 10 children for Joseph, but alas some of them had died at birth, in infancy (including another baby "Joe"), or much later (as in the case of my late aunt Martha and uncle John, during their teenage years). At any rate, according to Uncle Willy, it appears that the strain of having to try to operate within a "three-party marriage" (or a *ménage à trois* with two separate houses) eventually told on Catherine - and she gave her husband Joseph an ultimatum of choosing between the two mothers of his numerous children. Joseph, evidently, chose the younger woman – namely, my grandmother Mary. Perhaps, therefore, it was not for nothing that she was known as "Babes"! Such a choice could not have been insignificant to Catherine's future health thereafter, and she was - according to Uncle Hammy - to pre-decease her husband Joseph. Uncle Willy, on the other hand, recalls that Catherine survived Joseph's death - but only by about one year or so.

(b) The death of my paternal grandfather, Joseph, and the marriage of my parents

Whilst I do not know the cause of Catherine's death, nor indeed exactly when she passed away, all three of my father's surviving brothers - Willy, Tom and Hammy - as well as Hammy's wife, my aunt Amelia, recall exactly when my grandfather, Joseph, died. This is because of the correspondence of that death with another major happening in the Joseph Bradshaw-Mary Ryan household. That other event was previously arranged marriage, for the following day, of the fourth son of that union or "partnership" - namely my father, James Bradshaw - to a lady who was named Margaret Ann Carty (otherwise, then, simply known as "Tanna" to her family and friends, and later known to John and myself as "our Mum"). In other words, my grandfather Joseph died *on the eve of the very day on which my father and mother were to marry*! That is not therefore a coincidental situation, or pair of dates, which any of my uncles, Willy, Tom or Hammy, are likely to easily forget – and, it seems, not one of them have ever done so.

So, when was that inauspicious date? The marriage certificate of my father and mother's wedding would, of course, be the ideal thing to have to hand as I write. For all three of my uncles, Willy, Tom and Hammy, confirm that, as a result of my grandfather's death on the very eve of their wedding day, my parents, of course, postponed what should have been their happiest day, in order to give way for the funeral of my Dad's father to take place. For, as noted earlier, in the Montserrat of that time, funerals normally took place within one day of the death of the loved one. Nevertheless, the (presumably, long-planned) marriage went ahead on the very next day after the funeral. It is, therefore, very easy to determine the date of my grandfather Joseph's death. It was just two days before my father and mother got married!

Alas, I do not have my father and mother's marriage certificate to hand. I do, however, possess a very good substitute – namely, my father's great family Bible, entitled "*The Holy Family Bible*", which was published by the Catholic Press Inc of Chicago in 1956. In this faux leather-bound tome, my father records, in his own handwriting on one of its first few pages, that it was "Presented to" him and my mother by "Brach of Bristol [on]…20.12.1958". Further on in the volume, he records, in his neat handwriting, some of the major events in his family's life - including the date of his marriage to my mother (see Fig 21 below). In relation to that major event in his life, my father is thus making the entry about his wedding day *ex post facto*. But I have no doubt that he would have recollected, and recorded with perfect accuracy, exactly *when* that event had occurred - even if he may, in part, have misspelt some of the participants' names.

So what does the relevant entry in my father's family bible say about his wedding? At the back of the tome, in the section entitled "The Life of Our Family", my father has filled in the blanks in his own handwriting. On the second page thereof, under the printed rubric "Marriage", the whole completed section, as shown in Fig 21 below, reads as follows:

"We J.A. BRADSHAW and M.A. BRADSHAW received from each other the Holy Sacrament of Matrimony on 15.9.49 at PLYMOUTH, R Catholic Church Montserrat

The priest who witnessed our marriage was Rev: Father Derridder

The best man and the bridesmaid who witnessed our marriage were
R.Riley, & CR. Cabey and Miss B Lench

GROOM'S PARENTS   BRIDE'S PARENTS

J.L. BRADSHAW   J. Carty
FATHER   FATHER

M.S. Ryan   M. Greenaway
MOTHER   MOTHER

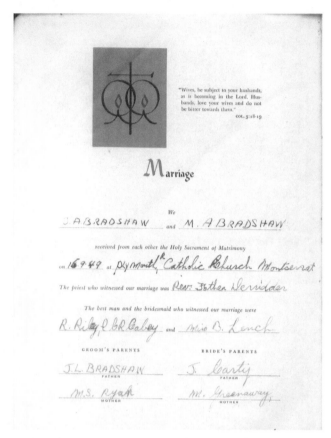

Fig 21: The details of my parents' wedding day – from the "Marriage" page of my father's family Bible

So there we have, what I regard as, firm documentary evidence of the exact date of my parent's wedding day – namely, the 15th of September 1949. It is interesting to note, by the way, that the number "5" in "15" seems to have been originally written by my father's hand as a "4" and then over-written with a more bold "5". This is some evidence, perhaps, that my father was thinking of the *original date* set for his wedding on *14* September 1949 - as he wrote up his family Bible some time after receiving it in 1958. As stated earlier, however, that original date had been postponed in order to allow the funeral of his father, Joseph, to first take place. Only when that sad occasion had occurred could the happier event then go ahead - on the day after its originally intended date, namely on the 15th of September 1949.

Fig 22: The photograph showing how Mum and Dad dressed-up on their wedding day – and depicting Mum's lovely "train for thought" and, according to my Uncle Hammy, posed in some garden in Kinsale, on the south-western coast of Montserrat. (Given the steps, and masonry, of the building behind them in the photo, however, could the shot have been taken outside the front entrance of St Patrick's R.C. Church, Plymouth? See Fig 15, in Chapter 2 above, for possible clues to answering this poser)

Fig 23: Another copy of the photograph in Fig 22 above but, alas, a damaged one – with Mum and Dad in "close-up", and without that "train" being in evidence

Thus, if my parents married on the last stated date above, it follows that the date of my grandfather Joseph's death was in fact the 13th of September 1949. For some time now, I have had in my possession the death certificate of one "Joseph Bradshaw" who is stated, on the document, as having died at

Dyer's aged 71 years. I had long assumed, from the time that the certificate came into my hands, that it related to my grandfather, Joseph, and that the reference to the date of his death as being "1986 June 27th" was somehow a mistake - a quirky error made by the Registrar General's Office in Montserrat which had issued the relevant copy on 28 August 1987. However, it suddenly struck me in the middle of the night recently that the certificate, in fact, relates not at all to my grandfather, "J.L. Bradshaw" (as my father refers to his own father in the former's family Bible) but, rather, to my grandfather's second son by Mary (and his namesake), and my Dad's brother, Joseph. In other words, to *Uncle* Joe.

But before completely putting to one side such death certificate as being not the most pertinent for the purposes of the present volume, there is at least one other fact mentioned in it which deserves our attention. It is the name of the "Informant" of my uncle Joseph's death to the Registrar of the relevant district of Montserrat at the time - namely District "C". This informant evidently signed himself, in the relevant Register of Deaths, as "Thomas *Bradshaw*"! This writer personally knows that there was a Thomas Bradshaw living opposite his (and my) uncle Joe's house at the time of Joe's death in or around 1986. This was no less a person than my first cousin, the late and great Montserratian cricketer and house-builder, Thomas *Bradshaw* - the son of my Dad's brother, and my Uncle, Tom *Ryan*. This shows, perhaps, that my cousin Thomas did not wholly agree with the stance of his father, and my uncle, Tom (or that of Tom's eldest brother, our late uncle, George) in being the only two "mavericks" of the family by calling themselves (in adulthood, at any rate) by their mother's surname of Ryan. Rather, that son of Uncle Tom, evidently, preferred to adhere to the line otherwise unanimously adopted by his father's, and Uncle George's, other brothers and sister and called himself "Bradshaw" - the surname of his "illegitimate" grandfather from Barbados.

(c) Further introducing Dad's brother, Tom

In carrying out my researches for this book I have, of course, spoken with other members of my father's family - in addition to Uncle Willy and, before him, Uncle Hammy, Auntie Amelia and their lovely daughter, and my cousin, Gloria - who are all, I am delighted to say, still alive and who were all born in Montserrat. Most important, in this connection, is my Dad's younger brother, Thomas - or "Tom" as most people almost always refer to him, unless one is from Montserrat where he would almost certainly be called "Ta-arm" in our local dialect. Of particular significance in this connection, is the long conversation which I had with him (and his kind, but "shy" (for that day only?) wife, and my aunt, Gloria) on Sunday the 2nd of March 2008 - which also happened to be Mothers' Day in Britain - at his home in Swindon, Wiltshire, in the English "West Country". We took the trouble of recording this conversation on film (despite Aunt Gloria's reluctance to appear on camera!), since it was intended to include references to "historically important" topics such as Tom and my father growing up together, along with their siblings in Dyer's, in the late 1920s and the 1930s. And given that Tom would be 80 years old in 2009, the opportunity was taken to record, on DVD, such historical "eye-witness" testimony - since such advantageous circumstances would be most unlikely to present themselves for too many more decades to come.

One of the most surprising revelations made by my Uncle Tom, during our recorded conversation, relates to where he and my Dad had gone to school. I had assumed that this had been somewhere very local to where their family home had been situated in Dyer's. And Dyer's, Tom reminded me, was somewhat in the middle of the island, and about 20 minutes by car in a north-easterly direction from Plymouth - on the road to Montserrat's old Blackburne Airport. But, to my question of which school they had attended, Tom immediately replied: "The Methodist School *in Plymouth*"! I then asked how had they travelled from Dyer's to their Plymouth school, and home again, during term time. Without batting an eyelid, Tom replied: "We walked! And if we were late, we found it better to run!" I then told him about my own BAREFOOT journeys to and from school, years after his and my Dad's own schooldays, and asked if it was the same with him and Dad. He confirmed that it had, indeed, been the case - but that, also like my brother John and myself in relation to St Patrick's RC Church, they had owned shoes (with which to walk from Dyer's in order to attend the Methodist Church in Plymouth each Sunday.

 Surprisingly, Uncle Tom told me that he could do the Dyer's-Plymouth distance "in just under an hour". I rather think that if a car needed about 20 minutes for the same journey, then Uncle Tom and my Dad must have been more running than merely walking to be able to travel the distance in under 60 minutes. (In this connection, Uncle Willy was later to tell me that "rolling a hoop" along the road on the way to school helped him to "speed up" and thereby arrive at school in time for its 9 am start). At any rate, unlike John and myself in our own Montserrat schooldays decades later, there would be no question of our father and his brother being able to go home from school for lunch - and then return for the afternoon classes, whether by merely walking or by road-running (even with hoops) *en route* back to Plymouth town.

But there is one thing that Uncle Tom's March 2008 testimony makes clear about his colonial schooldays. That is the fact that, one generation earlier than in the case of my brother John and myself in our Amersham hamlet, Tom, my Dad and their siblings in Dyer's village had also been "growing up BAREFOOT under Montserrat's sleeping volcano"! For, if we look at Figs 4 and 5 in Chapter 1 above, it is clear that Dyer's is much the same, near, distance (in a north-westerly direction), from the site of the island's 1995 Volcano in the Soufriere Hills, as is John's and my own Amersham situated to the south-west of that site. Accordingly, this book's main title also encompasses the childhood experiences of my father and his siblings, to a small extent at least, and, thus, further legitimises the place of this chapter within the volume's covers.

Uncle Tom, during our interview, went on to tell me about the time when he himself, and my father earlier, had just left school. This occurred when they were each, respectively, about 16 years old. And Tom also revealed that whilst he had begun his working life by helping (or continuing to give the help he must have started providing as a schoolboy, but at 16 supplied on a full-time basis) his parents with the cultivation of their Dyer's lands, my Dad had, instead, commenced learning the "trade" of being a carpenter. (Uncle Willy was to subsequently confirm to me that, at least for himself, school had to take second place to land cultivation in times of needful harvesting of crops, weeding of the land, and so forth). Thus, the respective working careers of Tom and Jim were different from the moment that they each left school, and such divergent paths were to continue for the rest of the respective time that they each continued to live in Montserrat. For Tom went on to tell me that although he did eventually leave his full-time agricultural work, in order to take up employment in a cotton-seed oil refinery in Plymouth, my father pretty soon began to pursue work opportunities outside the confines of the borders of Montserrat itself. Such openings were embarked upon, according to Uncle Willy, after my Dad had initially begun working in the carpentry trade in Montserrat (with one Willy Daniel) and thereby following in the footsteps of their own father. Thus, by taking up some of those, non-domestic, work "situations vacant" when they came along, soon after his leaving school, began for Jim the adventure of overseas travel. Such an urge or impetus to leave the safety of his native surroundings might well have been inherited by him from his own pioneering father, Joseph - who (we have already seen) had emigrated from his native Barbados to come to live in Montserrat, presumably in search of a better life. That same urge or impetus - or "bug", if you will - was, in turn, to infect my father's own children and grandchildren when they eventually came along years later.

(d) The travels of my father

As I write, I have to hand my father's first – and, perhaps, only - passport. It is stamped on its inside cover, and on pages 1,3,4,5, with the official imprint of the "Commissioner's Office, Montserrat" dated the 18th of

August 1945: see, eg, Fig 25 above. This shows that, by the acquisition of a passport at that date, my father was, at the very least, *contemplating* travel outside Montserrat by the age of 19 years. The photograph which appears on page 3 (see Fig 26 above) shows him to be about such an age - remarkably youthful and (dare I say?) good-looking, but with an air of seriousness, and dressed in a jacket and tie. Page 2 of the passport (see also Fig 26 above) gives his "Profession", as at the date of issue, as "Carpenter", his "Height" as being "5 ft 5 in", his eyes being "Brown", his hair "Black" and his "Special peculiarities" listed as follows: "Two slight scars above right eye". These "peculiarities" lead me to wonder, as I write, whether my father, too, in his youth may have had a particular liking for mangoes and whether he may also have had at least one too many set-tos with the native jackspanners also resident at Dyer's - years before I was to do the same with their cousins down at Amersham.

The front cover of my Dad's official travel document, that would open the way to his future trips "out of the island" of his birth, is embossed with the words "British Passport" as well as "Colony of the Leeward Islands": see Fig 24 above. In black ink are written the words "MONTSERRAT, B.W.I.", as well as the full names of my father. The former appear at the very top of the cover, the latter at the bottom. On page 4, on the pro-forma section which states "COUNTRIES FOR WHICH THIS PASSPORT IS VALID", the following is completed in handwriting also using black ink: "The British Empire" and "The Dutch West Indies".

Fig 24: The cover of my Dad's first, and only (?), passport - of 1945

David R. Bradshaw

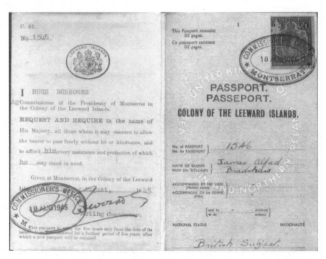

Fig 25: Inside cover and page 1 of my Dad's said passport of 1945

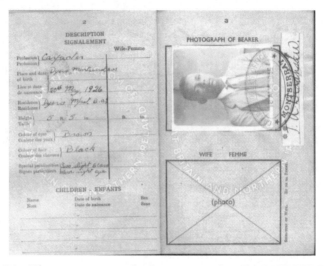

Fig 26: Photo page, and the personal, "DESCRIPTION", details (including "Special peculiarities") page, of my Dad's said 1945 passport

And it is in fact to the latter part of the world – or, at any rate, to the "ABC islands" portion thereof, near the north coast of Venezuela, comprising Aruba, Bonaire, and Curacao (see Fig 1, in Chapter 1, above) - that my father's passport shows him travelling to for, evidently, his first overseas voyage. For, on page 6, is a stamp from the "Netherland Consulate", situated on the neighbouring island of St Kitts - next to the words "Travelling to Aruba NWI ", which are signed off by the "Consul for the Netherland" and dated the 22nd of August 1945. There is then, on page 7, an exit stamp of the Leeward Islands Police, St Kitts-Nevis dated the 8th of September 1945, showing that my father spent a little time in one or other (or both) of those islands after first dealing with the Netherland Consulate. We then find, on the same page, an "IMMIGATIE [,] CURACAO, N.W.I." stamp, signed and dated the 11th of September 1945. Finally, we have evidence of my father arriving at his intended final destination in Aruba. For, on page 8, one finds two separate stamps purporting to come from a certain "DIENST", or service - more than likely to do with immigration - both signed, and both dated the 13th day of September 1945.

Why did my Dad go to Aruba for work? From my own knowledge, I am aware that his older brother, and my uncle, Joe, spent at least 20 years or more working in the oil industry in Aruba. This is because I met with Uncle Joe in 1979 and, in fact, subsequently did some "legal" letter writing, on his behalf, to his former Aruba employers in an effort to ensure that he received the proper amounts of pension due to him from the long years of service he had given to those employers. Thus, it may well have been that Uncle Joe was already working in the oil industry in Aruba when my father arrived there in September 1945 - and that one purpose of my Dad's visit, therefore, was to join him in that industry on a long-term, or even a permanent, basis. If that was so, then something must have gone wrong with this plan - for Dad clearly did not remain in Aruba indefinitely, since we have already seen above, in this chapter, that he was back in Montserrat for his father's funeral, and his own wedding to my mother, just four years later in September 1949.

Alas, there is no stamp in my Dad's passport indicating when he left Aruba after first arriving there in September 1945. There is, however, one which shows that he entered St Kitts-Nevis again on the 15th of April 1947. Could he have been on his way home after his sojourn in Aruba? If so, this would mean that he had only remained about 18 months or so in that Dutch territory - long enough, one might well think, to know whether or not he saw his longer-term future there - perhaps, working alongside his elder brother, Joe, in the oil industry of the Netherland Antilles.

Save for that 1947 (passing through?) entry stamp in his passport from the St Kitts-Nevis authorities, there is in fact no further stamp after the 1945 Aruba arrival until 1953 - some eight years after his first setting foot on Dutch territory. Nevertheless, I can distinctly recall my father telling me of at least one working trip which he had made to the United States of America - if not, indeed, of at least two such trips. Specifically, he had mentioned to me having gone to the mid-western State of Wisconsin in order to work there at harvesting apples. However, although my uncle, Tom, recalls at least one such work trip by my father to the States, he told me (during our March 2008 interview) that he thought that the venue of such temporary work had been the southern state of "Florida". So why is there no stamp in my Dad's passport relating to any such USA visit or visits?

The answer seems to be that the particular species of passport which my father possessed, as noted earlier, restricted its validity to "The British Empire" and to "The Dutch West Indies". Thus, insofar as he had travelled to the States for work, he must have done so using some other kind of travel document or permit. The issue then arises as to *when* such travel northwards from Montserrat to America had taken place. It is just possible that this may well have first occurred in the year *before* the 1945 Aruba trip. For although Uncle Tom told me, also in March 2008, that my father's Aruba jaunt had come before any American one, there is a tiny bit of evidence in existence tending to show, perhaps, that Tom may be mistaken in this aspect of his recollections. This evidence is contained in my Dad's copy of *"The Methodist Hymn-Book"* - the edition in question being that which was published in London by the Methodist Conference Office in 1933 - but which edition also includes a section entitled *"THE BOOK OF OFFICES[:] BEING THE ORDERS OF SERVICE AUTHORIZED FOR USE IN THE METHODIST CHURCH TOGETHER WITH THE ORDER OF MORNING PRAYER"*; which latter section was published by the same London publishers, in July 1936. I also have to hand, as I write, that little black book.

On the second page of the small volume just described, after its front cover, we see that my father has signed his name in his very distinctive, right-leaning and neat handwriting - which I still find readily recognisable, and moving, today. Just above this signature he writes a date - presumably that on which he was signing - namely "1944, 25 of may" (sic).

David R. Bradshaw

Just below his name, he also writes "Travalar's <u>Gards.</u> Amen;" (sic). So despite my father's unusual spelling - and we have to remember that he would have only just turned 18 years of age on the said 1944 date and been out of any formal educational system for some two years - this bit of writing is some evidence that my Dad was already a "traveller" at least one year before he set off for Aruba in August 1945. Thus, I am arguing that he may well have taken his hymn book with him on his travels (which could, perhaps, have been overseas to the USA), as early as May 1944 - because he regarded that little black book as being some sort of talisman, or, if you will, a "traveller's guard".

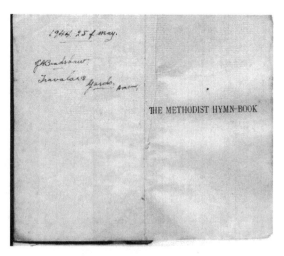

Fig 26A: Inside cover pages of my Dad's "...*Methodist Hymn-Book*", showing: his handwritten reference to (its being his?) "Travalar's Gards"; and his distinctive (1944-model) signature (which he was to maintain for the rest of his life)

(e) The original coming together of my parents, and their first transatlantic "separation"

We have already seen that according to the hand-written evidence of my father himself, provided in his family Bible, he was certainly back from his travels to Aruba (and possibly also the United States) by September 1949 - in time for his father's funeral on the 14th and his wedding the very next day. But, before those nuptials took place, one might well expect that there had to have been some sort of courtship period between himself and my mother, Margaret. One of the questions I had for my uncles, in relation to any such wooing interval, was: how on earth did Margaret and my father ever meet? I asked this because I already knew that she was a practising Roman Catholic girl living with her grandmother, Joanna, "down south" (of Plymouth) in the Kinsale area, whereas my Dad was a practising Methodist lad living with his parents some five or so miles north-east of Plymouth in Dyer's. So they were unlikely to have met at, say, a church social - for they went to denominationally diverse churches and lived in different parts of their island.

My March 2008 conversation with Uncle Tom was to provide the answer to my puzzle. For, according to him, my mother already had a female friend living in Dyer's when she first came across my father during one of her visits to that friend. Uncle Willy was, subsequently, even able to actually name that Dyer's friend of my mother-to-be. She was, in fact, a relative of my father and his siblings and was named Frances, or "Moom-ma", Ryan. She happened to be the daughter of one Thomas Ryan - the brother of their own mother Mary ("Miss Baby") Ryan. Thus, it is not difficult to see how easy it might have been for "Moom-ma" to have introduced pretty "Tanna" to her handsome, and as yet still-single, first cousin "Jim".

I asked Uncle Tom, during my March 2008 interview with him, whether, like the reverse of the Lady Diana and Prince Charles romance (which, as I understood it, had occurred only after Charles had already dated one of Diana's older sisters), my Mum may have "fancied" one or other of my Dad's five other surviving brothers - including Uncle Tom himself, of course - before turning her focus upon my Dad. To this, Tom replied immediately with an emphatic "No"! I am tempted to conclude, therefore, that whenever they had met in Dyer's, and howsoever was the occasion of their meeting, it must have been a case of "love at first sight"!

Since writing those words above in 2008, concerning my speculation about the 1949 (and before?) courtship of my parents, Margaret and Jim, I have met with a lady who knew my mother well during that earlier time. Indeed, she described herself, during my interview with her on Saturday the 6th of February 2010 at her home in Walthamstow, London – my first proper meeting with her since I was a baby in Montserrat! - as having been "really close friends" with Margaret at the time. Indeed, this claim is vindicated by the fact that she was chosen by my mother, or my parents jointly, to be my Godmother. For the lady in question is none other than the "Miss Herbert" referred to on the "Baptism" page of my father's bible (see Fig 7, in Chapter 1, above) – then more fully known as "Miss Maude Herbert", but today going by her married name of "Mrs Maude Brandt".

Godmother Maude was to tell me quite a lot about the varying characteristics of my parents when they were courting in that mid-20th century era – facets which I would come to know so very well within a decade or two afterwards. In short, whereas Margaret was a fun-loving girl "who loved to dance", Jim was a serious, very moral, no-nonsense guy who "did not like to dance"! Whereas, before her marriage, Margaret would go with Maude to various dances together, including the Old Year's Night one at the "Defence Force Club" in Plymouth, once she got together with Jim "he did not like her mixing with too many friends". However, Maude also told me, during our interview, that Jim regarded herself as "a special friend" who was allowed to come and visit Margaret at her home – even after my parents' marriage had taken place. Nevertheless, it appears that Maude still regarded my father with some caution – even describing him as being something of "a sly man" – because of his "strictness", though she is also clear that he was never a violent person when she knew him in those days. That "he had no sense of humour" is something that Maude remembers well. Moreover, his high moral principles stood out for her: "He kept to the straight and narrow. He was quite different from his brother, Tom, and their father. *I don't think he ever had another girlfriend apart from your Mum!*"

But whether or not Cupid instantly intervened with his bow and arrow, on the occasion of my future parents' very first meeting, we know that, at some point before the 15th of September 1949, my future parents, Margaret and Jim, must have decided to tie the knot and form a "legal union". But where were they to live after their wedding, when their respective parental homes were in such contrasting locations on the island - my Mum's near the southern seaside village of Kinsale, my Dad's distinctly landlocked and situated well-inland (towards the centre of the island, in the hilly Dyer's region situated on the Plymouth to Blackburne airport road)? This question was evidently resolved by a compromise - a re-location to a new place somewhere about half-way between the two parental homes (if you are travelling by road, as opposed to flying by crow). This new place was to be Ryner's Village - which, though north of Plymouth, was no more than a few miles from Kinsale and Dyer's respectively. But according to Uncle Tom, if my Dad bought or leased some land at Ryner's Village, for his future matrimonial home there, he still had to acquire "the home" itself. (In fact, Uncle Hammy was to tell me, subsequent to my interview with his elder brother, Tom, that my father merely decided to live on land that had been owned by their father, Joseph, whilst alive). In the Montserrat of the time, the solution to the "house-hunting" issue was a fairly straightforward one. You simply went out and bought a home - that is to say, you physically acquired a "chattel house"! You then had to transport the structure, somehow, from its site at the time of purchase to its new required location. And according to Uncle Tom, again during our March 2008 interview, this is exactly what my father did. He bought a chattel house, situated in St George's Hill, from its owner there and then had it transported, on the back of "a truck", to its new location in Ryner's Village. This tells me that my mother and father's first marital home could not, therefore, have been a very spacious one - and, certainly, like my future infants' school at St Augustine's, Plymouth, it would not very likely have had a flushing toilet system!

Fig 27: Photograph of a chattel house "on the move" in Montserrat sometime around 1983 or earlier. The house is probably a smaller version of that in which the author lived with Joanna, Maas Bab and his brother, John, whilst growing up on that island from the mid-1950s). The photo is used with the kind permission (and, indeed, positive encouragement) of Mrs Hanna Dale – the widow of the late Mr David Kenneth Hay Dale, former Governor of Montserrat (1980-December 1984)

Despite the absence of a functioning WC and (no doubt) other amenities, which any newly-married couple might take for granted in the 21st century, my parents must have been fairly comfortable in their little chattel house in Ryner's Village. For, just after the third anniversary of their wedding day, my Mum gave birth to me in that home on the eighteenth day of September, 1952. And, as will be seen shortly, within one year of that happy event, my Mum was to become pregnant again with my future little brother, John.

Between their wedding in 1949 and my birth in 1952, it is possible that my father may well have travelled to the United

States for one or more of those fruit picking trips there (of which, as I stated, he spoke to me during his lifetime). But I have argued earlier that he may have gone to America also, or for the only time(s), before his marriage to my Mum and even as early as in May 1944 when he was just 18 years old. But if that earlier argument is a mere indulgence in speculation, what is a provable fact is that, even if he had indeed (also?) travelled to America for work after his marriage in 1949, my father was certainly back in Montserrat again on the 17th of November 1950. For, on that 1950 date, he renewed the passport which we mentioned earlier and which took him to Aruba in 1945. On page 5 of that official document, the Commissioner's Office, Montserrat has made its imprint, just above two Leeward Islands stamps - each containing the head of King George VI and each to the value of two shillings. Next to this set of stamps, the "Commissioner" - one Charlesworth Ross - has signed his name and has endorsed the entry with the said 1950 date. Above his signature, he has written the following, in blue ink: "This Passport is hereby renewed [.] Valid until 18th August 1960".

Again, since writing the above section in 2008, my Godmother, Maude (*née* Herbert), has been able to confirm to me that working trips by Montserratians to Wisconsin, USA (in order to pick apples there) did, indeed, take place. Her testimony is based on her personal knowledge that her late brother, Thomas (also known as "James"), had been one of those migrant, but temporary, workers to that particular American state. What she could not tell me, however, was whether or not my father ever accompanied Thomas to Wisconsin for such fruit-picking ventures and, if so, during what specific year (or years) such working visits were made.

And, alas, Thomas is no longer alive to be able to tell us himself.

Despite its 1950 renewal, there is no evidence, within the passport itself, of my father having used it again - whether inside or beyond the British Empire or the Dutch West Indies territories - until some three years later. For, on page 9, we find some words which must have been just wonderful to behold for my pioneering Dad, namely: "Travelling to the United Kingdom". Underneath these hand-written words is a stamp, in the shape of a square box, imprinted by the "LEEWARD ISLANDS POLICE [-] Port of Plymouth, Montserrat". Just one other word is to be found within the said square box, namely: "EXIT".

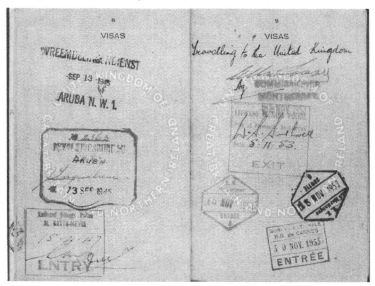

Fig 27A: Copy of pages 8 and 9 of Dad's passport (issued in 1945) – showing, among other things, the date of his "EXIT" from Montserrat (for "Travelling to the United Kingdom") on the 5th day of November 1953

The stamp in question is signed by hand and dated "5.11.53" (see Fig 27A above). So, there we have it! My father left my mother and me behind in Montserrat on Guy Fawkes Day 1953 - that is to say, *well before my brother John was born in May 1954!* Indeed, I myself would only have been just over one year old at the time.

From these last facts, it seems clear that my father's pioneering spirit, or perhaps his feeling of being impelled to create an adequate life for his small (but growing) family - especially given the reality that he now had a second baby on the way - took the greatest priority in his life. How difficult a decision it would have been to leave his dear wife and baby son behind (so as to chase a potentially happier, and more economically better-off, life in England) is difficult to guess at now. But at any rate, by November 1953 or sometime earlier, he had (with perhaps the encouragement of my mother, his wife of just over four years by the time of his emigration) made the decision to leave his native island behind and take his chances in first world Europe.

The question arises, of course, of why my father chose England over the United States (with which latter place he was already familiar, from his apple-picking ventures) as the country in which to seek his fortune in late 1953. Could the answer be provided by the following passages from Professor Carol Tomlin's book *"Black Language Style in Sacred and Secular Contexts"* (1999)[8]:

"During the early years of the Second World War, Black workers were incorporated into the [British] workforce. Britain also opened its

---

[8] Published by the Caribbean Diaspora Press, Inc, Brooklyn, New York – with a "Foreword" by Dr J.A. George Irish (a native of Montserrat).

doors to a number of different nationalities, including their European neighbours and American soldiers, many of whom were Black….

Immediately after the war, many Black soldiers were shipped back to their respective islands. However, some remained and were joined by increasing numbers of Caribbean people who came to Britain to fill the labour gap in the post-war period. In 1951 there were some 15,000 Caribbean newcomers. **America had been the traditional destination for Caribbean people but their entry [w]as restricted because of new legislation, most notably the 1952 McCarren-Warren Act.** *Therefore, Britain became the natural focus for migration.*" (See pp 36-37. Emphasis added).

Some sort of legal barrier, therefore, may have prevented my father from emigrating to Wisconsin - or any of the other, then, 47 or so United States of America – in 1953. But after departing Montserrat on the 5th of November of that year, page 9 of his passport shows that he had to pass through the French island of Martinique, to the south, *en route* to his chosen alternative goal of Europe. For we see, on that page, both "ENTREE" and "SORTIE" stamps for that French island, both dated the 15th of November 1953 - thus evidencing the likelihood that my father did not hang around long enough to be able to sample many of the delights of the territory offered by the birth-island of Napoleon's wife, Josephine. This, presumably, is because my Dad had a boat to catch! That is to say, that he probably only went to Martinique in order to pick up an onward French ocean liner there. This is owing to the fact that the last stamp, on the same page 9, shows that he duly arrived in France on the 30th of November 1953. The port of his "ENTREE" is stamped by the "SURETE NATIONALE" as being "R.G de CANNES". That imprint, therefore, evidences the fact that my Dad first arrived in Europe on the Côte d'Azur - but, alas, out of the holiday season and, presumably, out of holiday weather as well!

But if the European winter temperatures might have daunted him on his arrival in the south of France, he still had the even more difficult task to overcome of finding his way from the Mediterranean region to the even colder channel ports region in the north of that country - and then over to his ultimate destination in England. The penultimate stamp in his passport shows that my pioneering father was able to accomplish his goal by first getting to the Channel port of Dieppe - despite the distance and, presumably, his unfamiliarity with the French language. What means of transport he used to get from Cannes to Dieppe is not recorded in his passport, but page 10 shows a stamp, in black, evidencing the fact that he made a "SORTIE" from that Channel port - presumably on a cross-Channel ferry - on the 1st day of December 1953. Then, on the same page, is the very last stamp itself. Alas, it does not clearly state that it emanates from an immigration authority in England. But the initials in blue clearly state "L-B" together with the number "5". One wonders, therefore, whether the "L" could be some sort of reference to his arrival in London? What is not in doubt, however, is the date of this last stamp - also given in blue - which is stated as "2 Dec 1953".

Thus, if my uncle, Joe, had been the first of the seven surviving offspring from the Joseph Bradshaw-Mary Ryan "partnership" (to use a modern expression for the "common law marriage" scenario) to leave Montserrat and re-settle in Aruba, Dutch West Indies, his brother, Tom, (much to my surprise) confirmed to me, during our March 2008 interview, that my own Dad had been the *first* of those seven to do likewise in relation to Europe - by emigrating there and establishing himself in a new permanent life in England. *What is more, the rest of the siblings all followed him - no doubt with my father's help - all, that is, except Uncle Joe* (who must have been content with his new life in the Netherland Antilles island of Aruba, which my Dad had either not liked or did not make the grade for emigrating into when he visited, and lived for a while in, that island from September 1945). Uncle Hammy, for example, told me during our March 2008 meeting that he, in turn, came to London by a boat journey from Montserrat to Genoa, Italy and then travelled on by train to the cross-Channel ferry port in Calais, France. He had arrived in London in May 1955, and his wife (my aunt, Amelia) joined him there some months later on the 2nd of December 1955 - exactly two years, to the day, after it appears that my father had made his own (probably unheralded) entrance into his very new (and, no doubt, alien and cold) life in London[9]. By then Uncle Hammy's brothers, George, Willy and Tom, had already arrived to join my father in the British capital. Only their sole-surviving full-sister, my aunt, Mrs Mary Martin (*née* Bradshaw), of the six siblings who were to settle with their individual families in England, came to London after Uncle Hammy. It is, thus, clear that his brothers and sole sister must have been (at least, a little) impressed by what my father had done in

---

[9] My father's arrival, and initial experiences, in England's capital city was, most probably, not unlike those of other fellow West Indians arriving there in the 1950s – as portrayed in Samuel Selvon's *"The lonely Londoners"* (published by Harlow–Longman 1985; and originally published by A. Wingate, London, 1956). His individual experiences, however - given his strict moral code, backed up by the shield of his Methodist "Traveller's guard" - would, no doubt, have been minus the loose sexual relationships so graphically evidenced in that book by some of the newly-arrived characters in Selvon's book.

David R. Bradshaw

emigrating to, and trying to establish himself in, England that they all - save for Uncle Joe - decided to "follow suit".

Fig 28: Mum and Dad together again – sometime in the 1950s (?), after being reunited in England (following their separation in Montserrat in November 1953. which lasted until Mum came to England to join Dad in or around March 1955)

(f) Dad "finds his feet" in England; and a new baby in his arms

I deliberately used the words "trying to establish himself in…England" in the last paragraph. For, it is clear (from what subsequently occurred) that my father, Jim, was not simply prepared to arrive in the capital city and let inertia set in. Rather, he must have been on the look out for any reasonable opportunity to better his nuclear family's prospects - whether such opportunity presented itself in London or outside of the metropolis. And, according to Uncle Tom, such an opportunity did indeed subsequently arise in the railway town of Swindon, Wiltshire - some 90 miles or so west of London, just off the old A4 road which runs from the capital to the former slave port, and city, of Bristol. This must have been sometime after the 6th of February 1956, for on that date my youngest brother, George Frederick Bradshaw, was born at the Hackney Maternity Hospital in London. George's birth date, however, at least attests to one important fact. That is, the great likelihood that my mother and father must have been back together (at least for a very short while), after their long transatlantic separation from November 1953, approximately nine months or so before George's nativity - that is to say, on or around the 6th of May 1955. In taking the time frame of my father's employment move to Wiltshire by reference to my youngest brother's birth date, I am assuming, of course, that my father did not wish, for a second time in his life, to leave my pregnant mother in one locality whilst he travelled to live and work in another - simply in order to get a head start in pursuing an opportunity to further the prospects of his expanding family.

The new opportunity in Wiltshire, according to Uncle Tom during my interview with him in March 2008, was with a Swindon-based firm called British Moulded Plastics, or "BMP". Such an opportunity was, in fact, given to both brothers - Tom and my Dad - and they both moved to Swindon to take up their new jobs. Interestingly, they maintained their independence of each other, once they had arrived in the Wiltshire town, by not setting up home together in the same household. Rather, my father began living with my mother and baby George in the Penhill area of north Swindon. Uncle Tom, on the other hand, along with his then wife, my late and wonderful Auntie Catherine or "Rose", and some of their children (with their other offspring, like John and myself, still yet to arrive from Montserrat) took up the tenancy of a house in Courtenay Road, near the Walcot district in south Swindon.

Such independence, in the two brother's approach to life's opportunities, meant that, eventually, when my father changed jobs for an opening in British Railways in the town, his brother did not join him there. Moreover, whilst Uncle Tom was to stay on in his council-provided property in Swindon, my father, instead, (around the time of his joining the railways) obtained a mortgage to enable him to purchase his own home at number 64 Gooch Street, Swindon - not many steps from Swindon's mainline railway station. It would be to that very railway station and, subsequently, to that very house that John and I would arrive - after first disembarking from the ocean liner, *Irpinia,* in Southampton on the 31st of August, 1961. What adventures we two brothers encountered during that voyage to get to that English port, what problems we then had to overcome in trying to arrive safe and sound at our parents' home in

Swindon, and what was the aftermath (which featured my very non-Montserrat-like school days in England), I hope to be able to chronicle in the very near future – "if God spares my life", as any true Montserratian might well say!

Fig 29: Photo of Mum and little brother, George, prior to (?) the arrival of bigger brothers, David and John, in England in August 1961. It was, most likely, taken outside the front door of No. 64 Gooch Street, Swindon, Wiltshire – the very first home of the two elder brothers in England